This Second Printing Of

"Sara's Blessing"

Is Dedicated In Loving Memory To

Edwin Langberg

(April 6, 1925 – December 10, 2006)

By His Sons

Michael David and Jonathan Jason Langberg

January 2007

Sara's Blessing is a suspenseful tale of a 16-year-old boy who quickly becomes a man when caught in the swirl of the Nazi invasion. This very readable and uplifting story shows a young man determined to take charge of his own destiny in gruesome times of oppression and to survive without the stain of collaboration with evil. One step ahead of the Gestapo and later the Soviet NKVD, he crisscrosses Europe to find freedom. The memoir is written in two voices: one, of a young man in his teens recounting his stark adventures and the second, by the same man in his seventies, trying to understand the historical context of the events, some of them little known and, even today, highly controversial.

"It helped me understand why six million people marched to their deaths with so little rebellion."

Sara's Blessing

Edwin Langberg

with Julia M Langberg

Emethas Publishers
www.emethas.com

To order this book, contact:

Emethas Publishers

www.emethas.com

For my sons, Mike and Jon

v

Contents

Contents

My travels 1942–1948

National boundaries
Historical boundaries
Sea
Rivers
Bridgehead
Travel by train
Other ground travel
Air combat and travel

Estonia

Latvia

Baltic Sea

Lithuania

Oder River   Vistula River
Elbe River   Poland

9 US Army   Rathenow   Bydgoszcz
May 1945   Torun
                Berlin
                        Modlin   Bug River
                        Warsaw

Germany

                        Lublin
            Vistula River
Czech   Katowice   Rov
    Pilsen
        Prague   Krakow   Galicia
    Domazlice   Tesin Cieszyn   Lvov
Regensburg   Republic   Drohobycz
                                    Stryi
            Slovakia   Ukraine
    Austria
        Hungary

Romania

© Edwin Langberg 2002

Grigoryevskoye

Yaroslavl — River Volga

R u s s i a

Moscow

Ryazan / Sielcy

Tula

Belarus

Pre 1939
Polish border

Kursk

River Don

Rovno

Kiev

Kharkov

Stalingrad — 220 mi

U k r a i n e

Vinnitsa — Water tower

Crossed frontline
here Sept. 1943 — Interrogation

Podgorodnoye

Dnepropetrovsk

Stalino

River Bug

Zaporozhie

River Dnestr

Moldova — Transnistria
Berezovka — Nicolaev

River Dnepr

Odessa

Black Sea — Crimea

Sea of Azov

Father in
Kazakhstan
~ 1000 mi ⟶

Acknowledgements

My wife Julie's contribution was essential in writing this memoir. Every word written here was bounced back and forth between us until we were both satisfied. Our method of "creative criticism" could never have worked without the loving bond between us, helping to resolve the sometimes stormy reaction of my injured "writer's ego." Her constant encouragement was invaluable.

The first draft of the memoir was distributed in email installments to a close circle of friends and relatives who became an enthusiastic support group. Among them I would like to especially thank Eleanor and Bob Hill and Dan Rossman. Following the first draft, an early manuscript was circulated and useful comments and corrections were contributed by Eleanor and Bob Hill, George Oscar Lee, Alvin Goodman, and Judy Ebbert. My late mother-in law, Julia Kozubal was a great source of encouragement. She is missed.

My son Michael D. Langberg made an important contribution to the memoir. He took time from his busy journalistic duties to edit the manuscript, providing many valuable suggestions that enlivened and clarified the text. He also wrote the epilogue to this memoir. Michael, himself a published book author, introduced me to the intricacies of the publishing world. His wife Debbie's meticulous eye caught quite a few errors that managed to sneak through. They named their daughter Sara after my grandmother, the spiritual heroine of this memoir.

My son Jonathan was a patient reader and a source of encouragement. His son Karl lifted my spirits by saying that the author of Sara's Blessing is the bravest man he knows. My other grandson Sam honored me by using the memoir for his sixth grade book report.

Part 1

A Year in the Ghetto

Chapter 1

A Night to Remember

The rhythmic beat of heavy boots marching east on the cobblestone street below my window kept me awake. The rhythm, interrupted only by the noisy clatter of mobile field kitchens and by guttural commands in brusque German, was like waves of water from a biblical flood engulfing me and all that I knew. I pulled the covers up over my head, but the sound persisted – tak, tak, tak, tak -- the troops marched on.

It was the late night hours of June 30, 1941. The town was Drohobycz. The country was the eastern part of what was formerly Poland, annexed to the USSR two years previously. The soldiers were the German Army that had attacked the USSR a week earlier. I was a 16 year old boy, known to my friends as Ed. Sleep was out of the question; I was too terrified. The night dragged on. "Ed, can I join you?" It was Sophie, our housekeeper since my mother died three years earlier. Sophie was in her middle thirties, pleasantly plump, and the subject of my secret fantasies since puberty. "Yes, yes," I whispered as she crawled in next to me. Although she was shivering, I felt the warmth of her body next to mine. Primal sex can be a powerful antidote to primal fear. As we embraced, the rhythm of heavy boots seemed to recede as passion took over. First sexual experiences are memorable and the passion of this one on the doorstep to hell certainly was. We both fell asleep in a tight embrace as the troops marched on...

Before that night in June, 1941, I was just a high school student, doing well in my studies. I was practically an only child since my sister Dvora was six years older and married. I was particularly interested in radio and telephone. I loved to tinker with electronic gadgets and eagerly read the few magazines and books that were available describing their operation. My favorite subjects at school were math and physics. In the summer, I played soccer and swam; in the winter I enjoyed skiing in the Carpathian foothills nearby. I was like any other boy: I stared into the mirror to look for my first whiskers and I worried if I would fall over my feet at my first high school dance.

In Poland, before the Soviet annexation in 1939, my family lived in a two-story tan stucco apartment house at 33 Mickiewicz Street. The building was built by and belonged to my mother's father, Zallel Nacht. My grandparents lived in one apartment, my uncle Elias and his family lived in the second apartment and my parents and I occupied a third unit. There were also two smaller apartments that were rented to non-relatives. I played every day with my cousin Theo who was also my best friend. He was my uncle Elias' son. His mother, my aunt Clara, patiently gave me piano lessons for years but I did not turn out to be a receptive or talented pupil.

This family life routine ended when the war began. World War II had begun for us two years earlier, on September 1, 1939, when Germany attacked Poland. Since England and France had an alliance with Poland, they honored it by declaring war on Germany. Within weeks, Germans overran the western part of Poland. The eastern part of Poland, including Drohobycz where I lived, was "liberated" by the Soviet Red Army, under terms (secret at the time) of the Nazi-Soviet Pact. How one fared under the Soviets depended on where one fit in the Soviet's all-important perception of "class." My father, an MD and a dental surgeon, was "working intelligentsia" and this entitled us to reasonably undisturbed lives.

Before the storm: - Family picture in 1937

Standing from left: Author (age 12), Sister-Dvora, Father-Samuel, Aunt Clara, Uncle Elias, Cousin Lillie, Uncle Isaac. Seated: Mother-Rosa, Grandmother-Sara, Grandfather-Zallel, Aunt Regina. Seated below: Cousins Ruth, Jael, and Theo.

On the other hand, a few days after the Soviets moved into Drohobycz[1] (pronounced 'dro HO bitch') in September, 1939, my uncle Elias Nacht was arrested by the NKVD, the ever-present Soviet political police, and then killed in their prison. His only crime was that as a local lawyer and supporter of Zionist causes in pre-war Poland, he belonged to the class of "capitalist oppressors." In Stalin's ideology, it was always good to kill perceived potential opposition leaders to terrorize the general population and so ensure obedience. In this, the Soviets succeeded well.

All of the members of my uncle's family, who lived in our apartment house, including my cousin Theo, his sister Lily, their mother Clara, and Uncle Elias' 65-year-old Viennese mother-in-law, Mrs. Neustein, were deported to a part of Kazakhstan near Siberia. The Soviets also "relieved" my grandfather of his ownership of his apartment building and moved him into the tiny basement apartment where he later died.

On June 22, 1941, Hitler attacked his pact partner, the Soviet Union. That night was the shortest of the year. Our whole family was awakened in the pre-dawn hours by loud explosions. My father tried to console us by saying something must have gone wrong at the oil refinery. We all went back to our beds.

I dozed but in awhile, a loud roar from the sky made me jump from my bed again. I opened the window wide and saw hundreds of airplanes flying into the light of the sunrise. I ran to my father's desk and grabbed his binoculars, waking him in the process. Together we saw the unmistakable black crosses of the *Luftwaffe* on the wings of the airplanes. I looked at my father wide-eyed and shivered; he somberly put his arm around me. The conclusion was inescapable. The epic battle between the Nazis and the Soviets had begun.

At daybreak, we turned on the radio and anxiously awaited the 6 a.m. news. First, came the local news which included the usual propaganda reports of the achievements that the Soviet farmers and workers made in exceeding their production quotas: What a time to hear that the harvest was ripening ahead of schedule and factory production was humming. Next, came the war news, but not from here but from Syria and England:

When we finally thought we would get some real news, instead we heard the morning calisthenics class on the radio: "Stretch your arms and hold... one, two, three, four. Good! Try again and stretch your arms; hold... one, two, three..." We were speechless at this macabre denial of reality.

The bloodiest war in history had begun; 20 million Soviet citizens were destined to die and Stalin still did not get over his paranoia. He was been warned by Churchill and Roosevelt of the impeding invasion. Even I could see the flights of German reconnaissance planes almost daily. Stalin did nothing, convinced that the "Western provocations" would go away. That night he was unable to admit that he was not the *all-knowing genius* that his propaganda had made him out to be. He could not admit the incredible blunders of his bloody purges of the Red Army commanders, of his pact with Hitler in 1939, of his stabbing of Poland in the back, and of his sending Drohobycz oil to fuel the German invasion of France.

That night Stalin, disbelieving the news from his front commanders, insanely issued orders to his troops not to provoke the Germans and not to shoot at them. In the meantime along the five-hundred mile front, the Germans seized undamaged every bridge that was essential to their tank strategy. By midday, the Luftwaffe knocked out twelve hundred Soviet warplanes while loosing ten of their own. Soviet headquarters, communication centers, and ports were bombed. It was only the vastness of Russia that spared the Red Army from total collapse from the initial German blow.

In that chaotic last week of June, 1941, we were all stunned by the speed of events. My father was quickly inducted into the Soviet Red Army because he was a medical doctor. Moshe Laufer, my sister's husband was a pharmacist and was also called to serve. Both men were ordered to report to a Soviet Army hospital for duty. My sister managed to join her husband.

My grandmother encouraged me to get out of town with the retreating Soviets, but I couldn't. I spent 24 hours on a civilian evacuation train that never left the station. Then, a distant cousin who fancied himself an automotive expert got hold of a junked truck. We worked on it for several days, but we weren't able to get it started. Even if we had, gasoline was next to impossible to obtain and railways and roads were the favorite target of the German *Stuka* dive-bombers. We knew that our odds of getting out alive were far from certain, but from listening to Hitler's tirades on the radio, we also knew these odds were much better than the ones Hitler gave the Jews.

In the last days of the Soviet presence, the army hospital that my father was assigned to was evacuated into a train. I went to the railway station to say goodbye to my father. What I saw was a long row of boxcars, filled with wounded Soviet solders lying in their blood-soaked uniforms on the straw-covered floor of the boxcars. I finally found my father but I never did see my sister and her husband leave that day. My father and I both knew that it was too late for me to get out. "Take care of Anatol for me," my father sadly whispered, and he gave me his gold watch. As the train pulled out, we both sensed that perhaps we would never see each other again.

I was left behind.

Suddenly, I realized the crushing weight of my father's request. I was now in charge of what remained of my family: my grandmother Sara, crippled by arthritis; her nurse Blima; my stepmother Tova; Tova's one-month old infant son, Anatol; and our former housekeeper, Sophie.

Chapter 2

The Noose Tightens

In those first few days of the German occupation, frightening news came that some Ukrainian inhabitants of our town rioted, killing many Jews and looting Jewish stores. Our apartment was in one of the ethnically mixed and best residential parts of town and the riots did not reach us. But 47 Jews were killed in the Jewish neighborhoods and 250 more were seriously injured. Many of them died painfully without being able to get medical help. The German military commander then issued an edict forbidding further murder and establishing relative order.

By early July, Germany's political police -- the Gestapo -- arrived. One of the first things the Gestapo did was to find the chief rabbi of our town and instructed him to select a half-dozen people to establish a "Judenrat"(pronounced YOU-den-rat), which means Jewish Council in German. The men selected for the council were well qualified to represent the Jewish community. The council was comprised of intelligent, well-educated, pre-war Jewish community leaders, fluent in German, who had mostly fallen on hard times during the previous two years of Soviet occupation. In our town, Dr. Isaak Rosenblatt, a lawyer, headed the Judenrat. He in turn appointed his son-in-law, Maciek Ruhrberg, a struggling young lawyer before the war, as his second in command.

It was made clear in official announcements that we were to obey all orders of the Judenrat. We were ordered to wear white armbands with a blue Star of David on our right sleeve. Next we were ordered to walk only in the street, never on the sidewalk and to bow to uniformed Germans. This made me feel like a walking target. My immediate domestic job was to consolidate what was left of our family and our belongings into one apartment. I moved my grandmother Sara and her nurse, Blima, out of the basement and into our apartment on the first floor. We were more crowded but comforted to be together.

The Judenrat had quickly become a sizable organization, housed in a large three-story building that included its own police force. My first order from them came from their Work Office, called the *Arbeitsamt*. All male Jews ages 16 to 65 were to report daily for a work assignment. Of course, my formal high school education ceased. I would get up at 6 a.m. and report to the work office yard, a few miles away, to be marched off to my assignment. I don't remember much about the work yard, but I do remember a little balding Jewish man named Mr. Herzig who was the head of the Work Office. He and his underlings herded us around into work crews. To me, it looked like he relished his power and took pride in his newfound importance.

For the first couple of months, I dug up and loaded crushed asphalt chunks onto railroad flat cars. One day, a big asphalt chunk fell on my right big toe and smashed it, but there was no time off for recovery. That was too dangerous. The Ukrainian foremen could easily beat one bloody. Our pay for hours of work was one quarter of a loaf of black bread and watery soup at lunch. The official food rations were completely inadequate for survival. So in my "spare time," I traded our family belongings on the black market for food. There were several places in town where farmers from nearby villages would bring food on their horse-drawn carts and town residents would buy or barter their belongings for food. Later, when Jews were confined to the Ghetto, they could no longer participate in this trade.

SS *Hauptscharführer* Felix Landau, the Nazi in charge of Jewish affairs in Drohobycz, was our nemesis. (The ranks of Gestapo men typically ended in *führer* which literally means leader. Of course, Hitler used the title officially with a capital F in Führer.) In the middle of July 1941, my path crossed with Landau's when he came to our apartment, escorted by some Judenrat members to evaluate the merits of our apartment as quarters for Gestapo families. I was ordered to show him around the apartment. He was about thirty and I was 16. With his bull-like figure, polished boots and his form-fitting uniform, he radiated an unmistakable aura: "Look at me the wrong way, kid, and I will kill you."

Our apartment was spacious and, by local standards, quite modern. It had four rooms and a large kitchen. We had central heating, gas-heated hot water, and a modern bathroom. Landau liked our apartment and told the Judenrat to move us and all other occupants out of the building by the beginning of August.

Landau recorded his experiences at the beginning of the German-Soviet war in a diary. By a strange quirk of fate, the diary survived the war. Reading his diary and the duties he describes, I remembered that fateful day in our apartment. The uniqueness of Landau's diary is that he recorded with surprising openness and detail his feelings and motivation as the perpetrator of atrocities, at the time they were being committed, -- the same acts I remember from the point of view of a terrorized Jew, but more about his diary later.

In August, 1941, the Judenrat assigned us a dingy basement apartment at 20 Truscawiecka Street, near a stinking stream called Tysmienica that was more like an open sewer. The six of us -- myself, my grandmother and her nurse, my stepmother and stepbrother, and Sophie -- were now crowded into two rooms with a tiny kitchen. I had never realized what a lovely apartment my mother and father had until it was taken away.

We had to leave our furniture, linens, and kitchen utensils behind for the new occupants of our old apartment. Fortunately, we managed to take the rest of our belongings with us, as well as those of our now absent family members. This included their jewelry, clothing, pots and pans, knick-knacks and many instruments left from my father's dental practice. This meant I still had some things to trade for food.

I sent two registered postcards to my father's sister, Nettie Rossman, in Philadelphia. Because of censorship, the cards had to be written in German and contain nothing that reflected badly on the occupiers. .I was desperately hoping that relatives, whom I had never met, could find some way to send food parcels. Deaths from starvation within the Jewish population began to mount. My morale was kept up for a while by some vague hope that the postcards had gotten through to Philadelphia. Their reply was never delivered. Germany declared war on the U.S. and any hope for food parcels was dashed.

The memory of the circumstances of the postcards still shatters me to this day. My dear aunt preserved the cards and gave them back to me after the war.

In October, my work assignments changed for the better. The Judenrat was instructed to set up shops to produce items for the German Army. I was assigned to a shop (*Judische Stadtsgewerke*) that made cases and baskets for ammunition. The bizarre thing was that the shop was located in Blatt's Gimnazjum, our pre-war high school, and the Judenrat assigned many previous students to this location. The three-story brick building located along a side street in the semi-rural part of town looked the same on the outside, but that's where the similarity ended. The classrooms were emptied of desks, podiums and blackboards. The walls between the classrooms were knocked down to make it into a manufacturing space. We worked from 7 a.m. to 7 p.m. Still, this was light indoor work that was a blessing with the arrival of the cold autumn weather.

(Text translated from German)

Drogobycz, Sept 26, 1941

Dear Family!

I have not heard from you for a long time. How are you? I can tell you from here that my father, sister, and brother-in-law who worked in a hospital, have been taken by the Russians. I am left alone with my stepmother and four month old brother whose name is Anatol.

I do not know if my father told you about his second marriage to Tova Bussgang in the summer of 1940. We are all healthy. We have recently been moved from our apartment to another place. I enclose here my new address.

Please answer me soon.
With heartfelt regards,

Benjamin Herbst, my best friend and former classmate at the high school worked next to me in the shop. For a 16-year old boy, he was little. He was a wiry redhead and the nicest guy. Benjamin was not typical of the students in my class who were from well-to-do families. Blatt's Gimnazjum before the war was a private school and I imagine the tuition was fairly high. He never told me, but he must have had some sort of scholarship to attend the school. I had been to his house and it was clear Benjamin's parents were poor and couldn't possibly afford the tuition.

Now Benjamin's family was on the verge of starvation. They ran out of things to barter. My bartering situation was better, so I tried to have something extra for him to eat each day at lunch. At work we talked mostly about food. I still remember a popular story:

"A very proper group of six friends met for dinner one evening. The hostess managed to prepare seven tiny pieces of chicken for them to eat. They all ate their portion with gusto, but when the hostess asked if anyone wanted seconds, they all politely refused. Then, the lights flickered and the electricity went out. There was a loud shriek...When the lights came back, there were five hands covering the leftover chicken on the serving dish, with a fork going right through them all!"

In the late fall of 1941, news started filtering in nearby communities about "resettlements". Resettlement was a Nazi cover story for the shipment of Jews to death camps -- a very thin cover story. Since no one ever heard from those resettled, to me and to others who did not choose to put their heads in the sand, the conclusions were clear and inescapable.

Of course, we did not have any hard facts. The existence of concentration camps in Nazi Germany, even before the outbreak of the war, was well known. Before the war, such camps were used by the Nazis primarily to imprison political opponents. We had no way of knowing this had all changed in September, 1939, with Reinhard Heydrich's plan for a Jewish "Final Solution." The now famous camps such as Auschwitz and Dachau, in addition to killing Jews, had an economic role to provide slave labor for the Nazis.

Thousands of inmates lived there and some of the inmates capable of work survived to tell the story. We did not know that in our own vicinity, the construction of pure extermination camps had begun with "Operation Reinhard." The names of these camps are not well known even to this day, for the simple reason that no prisoners lived or survived there. The first extermination camp, where most of the Jewish population of Drohobycz died, was Belzec. It was located on the Lublin-Lvov railroad line. At least 600,000 perished there. Once the construction of this camp was complete, there were only a few hundred workers there at any one time to maintain the killing facilities and to recover clothing and items of value from the dead.

In December, 1941, Germany declared war on the United States. Any hope for food parcels from United States evaporated. We were very much aware of Hitler's pledge that if a world war broke out – which, in his perverted logic, he somehow managed to blame on the Jews -- he would finish off the European Jews.

Jews had no newspapers and were forbidden to have radios. The non-Jewish population had newspapers fed by the German propaganda machine. Usually, someone somewhere would listen to the BBC (British Broadcasting Corporation) -- a capital offense -- and spread the news from the West. Thus we knew that Hitler had failed to take Moscow and his attack on Russia ground to a halt.

This was our only ray of hope and a wonderful surprise. Up until that point, the Germans looked unconquerable. What we had seen of the remnants of the Red Army did not look good to us. In one of my work assignments, we traveled in a truck to load some bricks. The Germans had converted a huge clay pit and brick factory located a few miles outside of town into a Soviet POW camp. There were no tents, no barracks, and Soviet POWs were herded outside like cattle, thousands and thousands of them. Work detachments of POWs marched under German guard. They were walking ghosts begging for food. As hungry as I was, I just had to throw them the piece of bread that I was saving for dinner. The death of Soviet POWs by starvation and exposure was the first round of Nazi mass murder in our town.

At the end of December, lightning struck the Jews. On orders from the Nazis, the Judenrat issued resettlement notices to one thousand Jews in Drohobycz. The Nazis gave the quota; the Judenrat prepared the list of individuals. Their first selection was strictly along socio-economic lines. The poorest one thousand Jews were collected by the Judenrat police (*Judische Ordnungsdienst*) and delivered for shipment. The row upon row of victims was pathetically carrying on their backs, the allowed 25 kilograms of belonging, wrapped in satchels made of sheets. The whole operation was performed quietly and efficiently. We now know the victims were shipped straight to the newly-built death camp in Belzec.

The day after that first shipment, I felt relief at being spared. My relief turned to despair when I found out my best friend Benjamin was one of those thousand victims. This memory of the collaboration between the Judenrat and the Nazis has tortured me for years.

How do I dare to call it collaboration when the Judenrat had presumably no choice? I dare because I saw what happened and I experienced it. I dare because I want to understand how the Nazis corrupted the Judenrat, left the Jewish population leaderless, and expedited the Final Solution. I will talk more about this tragic subject later.

With the death of Benjamin, I felt more than ever that this war was very much my war, but what could I do? For lack of courageous leadership, a generation of would-be young Maccabees was weaving German ammunition baskets and waiting its turn to be slaughtered. I resolved at least not to be one of the passive victims.

Chapter 3

Family and Retainers

Taking care of a household of four women and a child was not easy. Food and dealing with fear were my main problems.

On June 19, 1940, my widowed 48-year-old father Samuel had married 31-year-old Tova Bussgang from the nearby town of Kalusz. Tova was a schoolteacher and a fine person. Samuel and Tova's first and only child, Anatol, was born on May 29, 1941, just a month before the German occupation. You can imagine Tova's frame of mind with her husband gone to the Red Army and having a small infant to take care of in the middle of hell. She became dejected and helpless. Anatol was a healthy and active child who in normal times would have been a source of great joy, but having an infant in the ghetto was a great worry. If we needed to hide, how would we keep him quiet?

Well, hiding was not really much of an option, because my 75 year-old maternal grandmother Sara Nacht was frail and permanently bedridden. She relied on her nurse Blima for all of her physical needs. Our housekeeper Sophie helped in trading for food and took care of meals.

The status of Sophie and Blima was an anachronism, an indirect result of the orthodox interpretation of the Hebrew Old Testament relating to "mamzers," those born of an illegitimate union. The *Torah* states, *"No mamzer shall be admitted into the congregation of the Lord; none of his descendants, even in the tenth generation, shall be admitted into the congregation of the Lord"* (23:3). The circumstances of their births tragically precluded Blima and Sophie from any chance of a Jewish marriage and family, or membership in the Jewish congregation in pre-war Poland when Jewish life was to a large extent ruled by Orthodox Judaism. Female mamzers frequently entered into service with Jewish families, usually at a young age. There was no binding agreement but after a year or two, both parties considered the position lifelong. Sophie took care of the children in my uncle Elias' family, and after my mother's death, she became our housekeeper. Blima took care of my arthritic grandmother for years. They were not family in the usual sense but the idea of terminating their services would never have occurred to me. My stepmother Tova and Blima found the daily uncertainty of our lives hard to deal with and, as a result, they would get panicky and hysterical.

On the other hand, Sara maintained an amazing degree of courage and cheerfulness. Except for her right wrist, Sara was completely immobilized by progressing arthritis. She sat propped up by pillows in her bed in our dingy apartment. She spent her time writing in her diary or, with her eyes closed, quietly praying. She must have been in terrible physical pain, yet it was hard to even get an aspirin to help her.

My grandmother came from a prominent Drohobycz family. At the beginning of the 19th century, after the Napoleonic wars, her family left Lauterbach, a town in the Hessen province of Germany, and settled in Galicia. Lauterbachs were a respected family of Cohanim -- descendants of Aaron and biblical priests. The family was not particularly affluent until the middle of the 19th century, when oil was discovered in the vicinity, and a method of refining the oil into kerosene was developed in Drohobycz. The town, about 50 miles south of Lvov and 250 miles southeast of Warsaw in the Carpathian foothills, became the cosmopolitan center of the oil industry and oil brought wealth. Drohobycz was part of the Austrian province of Galicia from 1772 until reverting to Poland in 1919. In

1939, under the Nazi-Soviet partition of Poland, Drohobycz was included in the Ukraine where it remains to the present day.

Sara's best-known ancestor was her uncle Asher Selig Lauterbach (1826-1906), an industrialist, scholar, and philanthropist. His incisive publications on the state of Jewish education in Galicia in general and Drohobycz in particular had a significant influence on the beginning of secularization, a very controversial issue at the time. The age of enlightenment began to shine in Drohobycz, fueled by the newly invented kerosene. Asher was involved in the refining business, wrote many articles relating to the oil industry. He founded a Jewish hospital, a library and a reading room, and aided Jewish refugees fleeing pogroms in Russia.

The main synagogue in Drohobycz now:
This dilapidated, desecrated, and decaying building stands as a symbol of the devastation to the once lively Jewish community there.
(Photo M. Wolter)

Sara Lauterbach married Zallel Nacht, a successful financier, and they had three children: Elias, Rosa, and Regina. Sara felt great anguish because of the sad fate of her family. Her husband died in 1940 of a stroke; her son Elias disappeared in a Soviet prison. Her youngest daughter Regina became an idealistic Zionist and moved to Palestine in the 1920s.

My mother, Rosa Rachel, was born in 1893 and died in 1938 when I was thirteen. Rosa suffered from depression, which at the time was neither understood nor treated. During the hot summer of 1938, my mother went on vacation alone to the Polish spa, Krynica. Within a week, my father was notified that my mother was in a comatose state. He rushed there and brought her back home. She never recovered consciousness and died within a few hours after returning home. I was told the cause of death was a stroke. I don't remember saying goodbye to her the day she left for vacation. Somehow, I came to believe she may have committed suicide with an overdose of sleeping pills.

My parents' marriage was not a happy one. I was too young to understand the specifics, but I have a clear recollection of their arguments and my mother's tears. She thought of leaving my father and moving in with her sister Regina in Palestine. In 1937, she asked me if I would like to go with her. I was closer to my father and I didn't want to leave him and my home. With horror, I remember my answer: "No way." Children can be cruel.

My grandmother, until her last moments, was a sweet and gentle person with a clear, intelligent, and incisive mind, and a loving and understanding heart. I cannot recall her ever raising her voice. We, her grandchildren, always listened to her, respected her and, above all, felt great love and affection for her. Under the tragic circumstances of the ghetto, when the world was collapsing around us, she showed inner strength and a stubborn vision of a happy ending for me that, under the circumstances, were hard to comprehend. The two of us spent many hours talking by her bedside. She told me with deepest conviction that she knew I was going to survive the war and have a good and long life afterward. She

19

taught me I must not settle for seeking only my own safety without helping those around me. She convinced me my life must have a purpose to be worth saving.

My grandmother's diary was a little book about five inches by seven inches, bound in blue velvet. She wrote in German and Polish. Here is a translated extract:

September 2, 1941:

"My life now is a living grave and my last removal from this cellar in which I live, to my real grave, will be a veritable salvation. Only mothers, who have been afflicted by a fate like mine, can feel what I suffer. My husband has gone, I have no sign of life from my missing son, and I gather all my strength to live for the sake of the sixteen-year-old Edwin, my only remaining darling grandchild, so that he may have me, at least, for his company. I crave for his well being and pray that he may be preserved for me and be well, so that he can work hard to maintain himself honorably and look forward to a happy future, which he with God's help and thanks to his hard work is bound to attain. He is my only comfort and hope in my bitter life. I am the living proof for human endurance. I open my eyes in the morning and I see the miracle of being alive although the bodily, and more still the mental pains during the night, are awful and cannot be described. Woe is my hopeless life!

"It is my prayer that these few last words of mine be preserved, so that after my death they may, as far as the circumstances will make it possible, get into the hands of my dear children, as all my thinking and longing after them has permeated my bitter unhappy life until the nearing end.

Sara died quietly in her sleep in May, 1942, and was buried in a Jewish cemetery between her husband and my mother. In her last will, included as a part of the diary, she urges me to have the three graves protected by a heavy slab of cement. It seemed a premonition: A year later, on order from the Nazis, the cemetery was bulldozed and the headstones were crushed and used for road construction. I could not manage to get the cement slab, but in any case, the slab would not have protected the graves from desecration. There is nothing left of the cemetery now, although some remains are probably still there, deep underground. After her death, when I read her diary for the first time, I realized Sara shared her pain and despair with her diary, while with me she shared only her courage. For me she was a tower of strength and hope. She somehow convinced me that with her blessing I would survive the war. She gave me the courage and determination to try. She was my inspiration for my fight for freedom.

I kept Sara's diary throughout the war and many years later, as she wished, gave it to her daughter Regina in Israel. The diary is now in the possession of my cousin Lily Gaulan who lives in Jerusalem.

Chapter 4

Preparations for Survival

After my grandmother's funeral, I had to report to the Judenrat for a housing reassignment. Now that there were only four adults and a child, the Judenrat assigned us to an even smaller one-room apartment. There was another reason for the reassignment: The Nazis had drawn plans for a geographic "sorting" of the population along ethnic lines. Pre-war Drohobycz had some 38,000 inhabitants, about half of whom were Jewish. Now, the still surviving 12,000 Jews were to be moved to a section of town consisting of just seven streets, perhaps 10 percent of the town's area. The object of this Nazi game was to create a strictly segregated and closed ghetto, a trans-shipping point to gas chambers. The closure with barbed wire fences was completed after I was gone.

Bartering belongings for food continued to keep us from starvation. But food prices were getting higher and our remaining stash of belongings was getting smaller. By the end of June, 1942, I had sold all of the family jewelry, clocks, china, quilts, shoes, clothing, and all other family keepsakes that were not absolutely necessary to survive, with the one exception of my father's gold watch. The meager diet took its toll on my budding sex life. Sophie was no longer pleasantly plump. She was now skinny and haggard looking. She would not let me touch her and I was too hungry to care. She withdrew; we did not talk much and became distant.

There wasn't much to carry when we made the move to our new hovel after my grandmother died, except for two large travel trunks that belonged to Mrs. Neustein, my uncle Elias's mother-in-law, who had been deported to Kazakhstan in 1940. Up until now, the trunks were well hidden and remained unopened. We had hoped she was living somewhere on a collective farm in Kazakhstan. I thought the time had come to break into the trunks, even if they did not belong to us. If I needed to rationalize, the trunks took up a disproportionate amount of room in our new apartment.

With a hammer and a large screwdriver, I forced open the trunks. I could not believe my eyes. I discovered exquisite tailor-made fur-trimmed garments, satin sheets, fine lace shawls, silk handkerchiefs, slips, scarves, fine handbags, stockings and beautiful shoes. On the bottom of the bigger trunk was a strongbox that resisted my efforts to open. The next day, I borrowed a hefty sledgehammer and a crowbar and managed to break into it. The contents were breathtaking: gold, silver, diamonds, garnet and pearl jewelry, including rings, bracelets, necklaces, hair combs, pins, broaches and gold coins. To top it all off, there was a little velvet-lined box holding a cut but unmounted sparkling diamond. It was the size of a lima bean. "Thank you Mrs. Neustein, there will be sausages for dinner tonight!" I shouted.

We were rich! With the newfound treasures, I could now see options. I could make provisions for my stepmother and my infant brother Anatol and for Sophie and Blima and for myself. I needed to find a Polish farmer who, for a good share of our worldly goods, now much enlarged, would hide Tova and Anatol. I would also give some of the treasures to Sophie and Blima and let them fend for themselves. For myself, I wanted to escape, escape, escape. I wanted to escape from being a Jew prepped for slaughter, escape from being a 17 year old that was responsible for everybody, and escape to even my score with the Nazis.

To implement my plans, I needed to have contact with Poles in order to buy papers to establish a Polish identity. Reading about this today, it may seem distasteful that the saving of Jewish lives by a non-Jew involved a financial transaction. But helping Jews by hiding them or supplying them with false identity papers, if discovered, involved prompt execution of all parties involved. In helping a Jew, a Pole not only risked his own life, but the life of his entire family. Genuine outside help, whether money exchanged hands or not, was an act of great heroism even if it was commingled with a little greed. Any help without financial initiative was an act of sainthood and God knows there aren't many saints.

I contacted some pre-war Polish classmates. Poles whom I knew personally were generally friendly and helpful. On a mob level, Polish anti-Semitism and Jewish anti-Polonism are legendary. But to me, the relationship between the Poles and the Jews in Poland was like the relationship between two brothers who thoroughly hate each other, yet know there is a strong bond there, somewhere. In this case, there was a half millennium of coexisting in the same country and suffering from the same oppressors.

My feelings toward the Ukrainians were quite different. Having had little contact with them on a personal level made it easy for me to see them as a stereotype: simple-minded and brutish. I remember the warm welcome the invading German Army received from the Ukrainians, their young women dressed in their Sunday best, greeting the invading Germans with flowers. How could they do this when Hitler's officially-declared conquest policy in the East was to enslave the local population including the Ukrainians? The black-uniformed Blackshirts, who were the SS-trained Ukrainian police, equaled in brutality anything the Germans had to offer and then some.

Part of my compulsory Polish school reading was a historical novel, "With Fire and Sword" by Henryk Sienkiewicz, a renown Polish writer. I have never forgotten his vivid description of Bohdan Khmelnytsky's Ukrainian Cossack uprising against Poland in 1648. Cossacks indiscriminately killed a majority of the Polish and Jewish population under their control. An estimated 100,000 defenseless

Jews perished then. I find it hard to stomach that to celebrate this rebellion that brought nothing but ultimate subjugation of the Ukrainians by Russia, the Ukrainian town of Proskurov was renamed Khmelnytsky in recent times, just to remind us that Ukrainians still cherish this butcher as their hero.

Of course, in 1941 I didn't see the millions of Ukrainians who fought the Germans in the Red Army or those who were trying to help the Jews. I fully realize now that my views at the time were just a part of the schism that propagates ethnic hate and distrust on both sides, so common in this part of the word.

Meanwhile, back at the high school making ammunition boxes, I started looking for escape teammates. Marek Schnepf and Fred Kreisberg were eager to participate. I knew them well from pre-war school days and skiing trips in the Carpathian Mountains. They were both a little older than I. All three of us were strong and athletic, didn't look particularly Jewish, and spoke unaccented Polish. Marek was probably the shrewdest of the lot. We were all eager to do something -- anything -- rather than passively wait for another resettlement.

Fred was the son of our family doctor and was well off. Marek's family was not in good financial shape, but this did not matter. We had enough money among us to get the Aryan papers we needed. Fred lived with his parents. Marek lived with his mother; his father had escaped with the Soviets. In any case, Marek and Fred decided not to tell their parents of our intentions until the plan jelled. Everything would be on a "need to know" basis.

There were two principal means of escape from the ghetto: hiding or assuming a non-Jewish identity. Hiding typically involved some arrangement with non-Jews to provide shelter and a food supply. Jews were hidden in basements, attics, and barns. Some hiding places were better than others. Four hundred hidden Jews survived the Nazis in Drohobycz. Escape under false identity required Aryan looks and unaccented speech.

Considering the centuries of cultural and social isolation between Jews and their neighbors, a surprisingly large number, maybe 15

25

percent of pre-World War II Polish Jews, were blond with blue eyes and otherwise hardly distinguishable in appearance from the rest of the population. If the coloring and features common to Jews and Arabs define Semitic characteristics, how can the fair 15 percent be explained? Inter-marriage is not the answer. It was virtually unknown, even in my day. One possibility going back to the 10th century is that the earliest Polish Jews were descendants of the fair Khazars. Crimea was on the Black Sea trade routes and some overzealous Jewish merchants converted the ruler of the Khazar Empire in Crimea to Judaism. When the Khazar Empire fell in 965, the Khazars moved northwest from Crimea, some settling in Poland. The other possibility has to do with wars, conquests, and pogroms that were more often than not celebrated with the looting of Jewish properties and rape of Jewish women.

Whatever the origin, an escape under assumed Aryan identity required non-Semitic looks. My fair skin, blue eyes, blond hair, small nose and good brain came from my father's family in Buchach, a small town some 100 miles southeast of Drohobycz. The Langbergs, a family of roofers and house builders, had lived in Poland much longer than the Lauterbachs but their past is not well documented. However, it is safe to assume that they, like most of the Jewish population in the area, moved from Germany in the14th century to escape a massacre of Jews caused by Christian religious zealots who misinterpreted the story of the Egyptian plagues in Exodus. They accused the Jews of causing the Black Death epidemic that decimated Europe. At the time, the Polish Kingdom was a safe haven.

Another prerequisite for escape under an assumed identity was unaccented speech. In Galician towns, Poles and Ukrainians spoke their respective languages. The dominant language of Jews was Yiddish, which originated as a mixture of German and Hebrew. In order to deal with the rest of the population, the Jews were invariably multilingual. Yet Yiddish has a powerful singsong quality that tends to accent its native speakers in any other language.

At the turn of the 20th century, the hold of Yiddish on the Jewish population began to weaken. Many of the intelligentsia strived to assimilate. They spoke Polish and German and sent their children to secular schools. At the other end of the spectrum were the orthodox Jews who spoke Yiddish, sent their children to religious Heders, where they would learn Hebrew and wear strange clothing that was once fashionable with the Polish nobility in the 15th century. I spoke Polish at home, and so I had a command of fluent and unaccented Polish. I picked up some Russian and Ukrainian at school under the Soviets. My parents, when they did not want the children to understand, spoke in German. This is a wonderful incentive for a child to learn a language. I also had some German at school, so I spoke tolerable German with a Polish accent. I could pass for a Pole.

The last prerequisite for a safe escape was an uncircumcised pecker. The "pants down" spot checks were a frequent and effective way to identify a Jew. At this time and place, there were no circumcisions except among Jews, so this method of detection was foolproof. I was vulnerable on this score; I had better keep my pants up.

I obtained a birth certificate and some expired food coupons in the name of Leslaw Strutinski. Leslaw and I were schoolmates in grade school. These documents were not much but they would have to do. I swore to him that if I were caught, I would confess to stealing the documents from him. Leslaw was the son of a pre-war Polish civil servant and his family was impoverished. I paid him for the documents, but this was really not commensurate with his risking his life. It was possible to get more elaborate identity papers with photographs and all kinds of official-looking German stamps, but they were fake, made by the growing industry of paper forgers in the Ghetto. I opted for modest but genuine papers. Leslaw instructed me on his background and family history and on Catholic ceremonies. I memorized the Our Father, Hail Mary, and Glory Be to the Father. I also learned how to bless myself with the sign of the cross and on what knee to genuflect. I studied this as if my life depended on it. It did.

For my own escape, I kept my father's gold watch, Mrs. Neustein's unmounted diamond, and a few hundred zlotys in cash. The cash would be enough to keep me going for a few months. I hid my Aryan papers, Sara's diary, and the cash under the floorboards in the apartment. I opened an electrical outlet in the apartment wall and put the diamond inside for safekeeping. A suitcase with my belongings was packed: a change of shirts, underwear and socks, shoes and work boots, a "Sunday" jacket and work clothes, an overcoat, hat, and gloves. I was ready to go.

My search for a Polish farmer to hide Tova and Anatol was a difficult business. The riskiest part was that the payment had to be made up front. How could I be reasonably sure that sooner or later the farmer would not dump or kill them? I couldn't very well ask for character references.

My best prospect was Janek, a farmer I had met at the market, with whom I regularly bartered food for our belongings. Janek was in his thirties. He was married and had five children and a small farm about ten miles from Drohobycz. He always acted sympathetic to the plight of the Jews. He was reliable and never tried to strong-arm me. Janek was also gutsy. Our black-market association involved a lot of risk to him. He was the one who got the merchandise in and out. I decided Janek was my man.

I showed him Mrs. Neustein's treasures that I allocated to Tova's escape and told him they would all be his if he solemnly swore to hide Tova and Anatol. Janek's eyes popped out of his head when he saw the goodies. He knelt and swore on all that was sacred to a Catholic that he would hide Tova and her baby. The deal was done.

A short time later, in the middle of July, 1942, Janek came in his horse-drawn carriage and loaded up Tova, Anatol, and the treasures that were now his. Anatol was a Darwinian favorite since he was not circumcised. The threesome drove off. I divided the rest of the treasure between Sophie and Blima. There was enough there to keep them bartering for quite sometime. Phase one of my escape plan was complete.

Marek and Fred were also ready. They decided the time had come to tell their parents. Marek's mother was sad to be left behind, but was very supportive. On the other hand, Fred's father, Dr. Victor Kreisberg, was harder to convince. He was a good friend of the head of the Judenrat and he wanted to have a face-to-face talk with him to ask about the real prospects of survival under Judenrat protection. Dr. Kreisberg convinced Fred to wait a week or two until they could meet. The escape date was delayed. I practiced, "Hail Mary, full of grace."

Chapter 5

Roundup

On August 17, I was on the second floor of the shop packing ammunition baskets into big bundles. Every once in a while, I would look out anxiously through the window at the pouring rain. Since yesterday, German SS and their Ukrainian Blackshirts were rounding up Jews for another death camp shipment. Some of us had stayed at work overnight since it seemed a lot safer than going home. Suddenly, in mid afternoon, I heard a commotion down the street, then shouts and shots. The downstairs gate for the building was knocked down and dozens of Ukrainian Blackshirts ran into the building. In a few minutes, they were on my floor. We were surrounded. They were beating us with their clubs, and yelling, "Get out you kike vermin! You'll be making baskets in hell!" A young co-worker named Miriam tripped and fell as we were pushed down the stairs. A Blackshirt shot her. There was blood everywhere.

We continued to be pushed down the stairs, about 100 of us, and out through the main gate. On the other side of the street, a German SS officer stood in the rain and directed the operation. The street was cordoned off about a hundred yards from us. The Blackshirts with their guns ready to shoot surrounded us on all sides while we waited. It took a while to flush everyone out of the whole building. I was full of adrenaline and only one thought swirled in my head: "They will not take me alive."

We were surrounded. I slowly inched my way through the crowd toward the side of the street. Finally, I was on the edge of the crowd between two Blackshirts who stood about 6 feet apart. A pavement separated me from a picket fence. I took a deep breath and darted out. I jumped over the picket fence, ran another 20 feet through a yard and into a field and heard a shot and the whizzing sound of a bullet. I fell down on the muddy ground and heard one more shot. I made a quick assessment and realized I was not hit. I jumped up and started to run again. I heard two more shots but they missed. Thank goodness for the downpour.

I ran another quarter of a mile through a field that surrounded our school. I knew where I was going; I had rehearsed it before in my head. I was going to hide in the culverts that fed the stinking stream of Tysmienica. One of the culverts was about 5 feet across, but there was one surprise. When I explored the culvert before, there was about one foot of water on the bottom. Now, because of the rain, the culvert was half full. It was hard to walk against the current of the stream, but I trudged onward. I was soon in complete darkness. I knew that in a few hundred feet the culvert would turn and split, and there I would rest. I wedged myself against the fork in the culvert and relaxed. Well, maybe relaxed is not the right word. From my jump over the fence until this moment, my actions were automatic. My feelings were shut off and a primeval fight or flight instinct was in control. I was now settling down to think and feel again.

My first thought was one of relief. I was alive and I was safe for the moment. Then, I felt pain in my left arm where I was hit by a club during the roundup, and then I began to feel fear. I was in a dark culvert. It was raining and the water was roaring and rising and death lurked on the outside. This was my first of many encounters with handling fear so that it did not turn into action-blocking panic.

This roundup had not been like the previous quiet, efficient Judenrat resettlement, an operation that followed a prepared list. The

Nazis were trying out their newly trained Ukrainian Blackshirts. This was an Action, or *Akcja* in Polish. It was a systematic house-to-house search, brutal dragging out of terrified victims, shooting those who could not or would not walk, loading the victims onto trucks bound for a railroad station, then pushing them into box cars destined for a crematorium.

After four or five hours in the culvert, I became thirsty. Drinking the culvert water was not an option. It was a sewer and a storm drain. I decided to wait another couple of hours to make sure it was completely dark before I would leave the culvert, reconnoiter and find some water.

Getting out was easy; the water current pushed me in a few minutes, but it was very dark outside and still raining. I could hear shots and screams, the roar of distant trucks, and I saw the beams of searchlights. The Action was still going on. I drank from the first clean-looking puddle nearby. I saw two new culvert segments that must have been dropped off for repair or extension. They were reasonably dry and clean, and I was very tired. I crawled into the dry culvert and dozed off.

When I awoke, it was daylight. I listened. It was quiet. It stayed quiet for a good long time. I was very hungry and cold in my wet clothing, so I decided to try to sneak back into our apartment, because it wasn't too far away. The neighborhood looked like a ghost town. The door of our apartment was wide open and I entered. Sophie and Blima crawled out from the narrow pantry where they were hiding. I stripped and washed from head to toe to get the smell of the culvert off me, and changed into dry clothes. We had something to eat and we exchanged our stories. Sophie and Blima were lucky. The Blackshirts had missed them.

In an hour or so, Marek showed up. We were both amazed and happy to see each other, and then Marek told me his story. They were all rounded up and driven to the railroad station. Maciek Ruhrberg from the Judenrat showed up and persuaded his Gestapo bosses to let the shop contingent go. That took guts. They were released, but the quota was filled by others and a total of the scheduled 2,000 people were shipped to gas chambers. Marek told me that Fred was with him during the roundup at the station. Fred was shaken but he concluded from the events that his father was right; the Judenrat could protect him. As a result, Fred said that he would not be going with us. There would only be the two of us.

We decided to waste no more time in leaving. Marek went home to get his belongings and we agreed to meet at Janek's wagon. I had already talked to Janek about giving us a ride out of town sometime. He told me to meet him where he did his black-market trading, and he would give us a ride in the afternoon when he was going home.

I said my good-byes to Sophie and Blima and went for my stash. I pulled out my packed suitcase and then opened the floorboards. I retrieved the birth certificate and the expired food ration book that would establish my new Aryan identity, the cash, my father's gold watch, and my grandmother Sara's diary. Then I got a screwdriver and opened the electrical outlet. It was empty!

The diamond was gone! I checked again and again. The outlet box was solid and the wires fitted tightly. There was no way it could have fallen inside the wall. There was nothing on the floor in front of it. I was stunned, but there was nothing I could do.

Marek and I met at Janek's wagon and we hid our suitcases on the cart. After the cart left town, we threw away our armbands with the Star of David and our Jewish identity papers. It was August 8, 1942. I was now Leslaw Strutinski, a Pole, and I had to believe it. It would be a very long time before I was Edwin Langberg again.

To give closure to my tale about Drohobycz, there are a few facts I must add. The Polish farmer Janek kept Tova and Anatol in hiding until December, 1942. In December, he dropped off Anatol on the steps of an orphanage that was run by Catholic nuns. The nuns took him in and baptized him as Maciek Grudzinski. Subsequently, Janek hit Tova on the head with an ax, but she survived. Janek could not bring himself to finish the job and ended up keeping Tova in hiding until the Soviets came in1944. Tova had a difficult time regaining custody of her son because the nuns considered him a Catholic and would not release Anatol-Maciek to a Jewish woman. Finally, in the spring of 1946, Tova and Anatol were reunited. The two of them left Poland for a displaced persons' camp in Germany and from there went to Israel. Anatol, now a professor of mathematics at Haifa University, and his wife Pnina, who teaches psychology, have a big, loving and talented family.

Tova reunited with Anatol in 1946

Fred was deported to the gas chamber at Belzec. Dr Kreisberg survived. I met him after the war in Poland and he greeted me with the bitter accusation, "Why didn't you take Fred along?" I did not remind him. He put his trust in the Judenrat.

What happened to the diamond? Your guess is as good as mine.

Chapter 6

The Judenrat Trap

It's a paradox of history that just about anyone with the least knowledge of the Holocaust has heard of Adolf Eichmann, yet few have ever heard of Reinhard Heydrich[3], the truly quintessential Nazi evil genius, the author of the plan to annihilate the Jews. Throughout his life, Heydrich was tormented by rumors that through his grandfather, he was "contaminated" by Jewish ancestry. Whether true or not, this undoubtedly contributed to his need to try to be a Nazi superman. He headed the SD and the RSHA, roughly equivalent to the Secret Service. In addition to this, he was an excellent violinist, an expert fencing master, and in his spare time from his office duties, he flew fighter-pilot missions in his specially marked ME109.

Around the outbreak of World War II, in September 1939, Heydrich was given the responsibility to form a policy regarding the Jews who were living in Nazi-occupied Poland. I cannot think of any other individual in history who had the task of planning the actual destruction of millions of people, not just their conquest or subjugation, but their actual execution. It is doubtful that the moral aspects of this gruesome assignment concerned him. His concerns were merely logistical: how can six million European Jews be physically destroyed with a minimum burden to the German war resources of men and material? A community on the verge of mortal danger needs leadership and inspiration to defend itself. A typical Nazi with less imagination would have opted for the destruction o the Jewish leadership as the initial step of this campaign. It was the

"Heydrich was a born intriguer, with an incredibly acute perception of the moral, human, and professional weakness of others. Unusual intellect, matched by the ever-watchful instincts of a predatory animal..."
(Walter Schellenberg, Heydrich's protégé and successor)

evil genius of Heydrich who decided to subvert the Jewish leadership to help in this task.

Heydrich's plan was clearly top secret. Only a few Nazi documents survive. From these documents and the events in the ghetto, a pattern emerges that sheds some light on Heydrich's Judenrat trap. On September 21, 1939, Heydrich issued a *Schnellbrief* (Accelerated Notice) to inform his commanders of the *Einsatzgruppen* SS and his Security Police of his assignment. The notice read in part:

"...In each Jewish community, a Judenrat, a Council of Jewish Elders is to be set up which, as far as possible, is to be composed of the remaining authoritative personalities and rabbis."

The Schnellbrief also pointed out the responsibility of the Judenrat to follow Nazi orders in organizing, implementing, and financing the clearing of the countryside and small towns of Jews and concentrating them in ghettos. He ordered the ghettos to be located in larger towns that were close to railway junctions. He also ordered a census of the Polish Jewry and survey of Jewish property.

In order to comprehend why the formation of Judenrats was such a masterstroke of genius, one has to look to Jewish history. Prior to World War II, the last historical evidence of a Jewish armed resistance was the Bar Kochba revolt in 132-135 A.D. which was brutally suppressed by the Roman Emperor Trajan. Some 500,000 Jews were killed and Judea was depopulated by a mass deportation of its inhabitants to different parts of the Roman Empire. When the Jews were sent into exile, the Jewish religion, as voiced by Talmudic Midrash, accepted that God, the Jewish people, the Roman Empire, and, by inference, the successor nations of the world, made a divine pact. One provision of the pact was that the Jews would not rebel against the non-Jewish world that gave them sanctuary; a second was that they would not immigrate en masse to the Land of Israel until the arrival of the Messiah. In return, the Midrash states that the Gentile nations promised not to persecute the Jews too harshly. By rebelling against this pact, the bulk of the orthodox Jews believed at the time that the Jewish people were engaging in open rebellion against God.

In the 18 centuries of Jewish diaspora that followed, the tradition of the Jewish community's survival was self-government in the form of Councils of Jewish Elders. The Jewish community survived hostility through negotiations between the Council and the oppressors. Naturally, this long tradition made the Jewish population trust the Judenrat and trust its role as negotiator with the Nazis.

As a first step after the occupation, the Nazis contacted a Jewish community elder, typically the town's chief rabbi, and asked him to produce a list of candidates for the Judenrat for Nazi approval. Considering the historical Jewish tradition, this did not seem inappropriate. In the beginning, the concerns of the Judenrat were perfectly legitimate, namely the problems of running a community in extremely trying circumstances, including housing, distribution of meager food, and medical services. The initial act of joining the Judenrat did not appear to be traitorous by any standard. When the German occupation started in Drohobycz in 1941, there was no doubt in anybody's mind that Jews would be oppressed, but there was no clear indication that Hitler had made up his mind that the oppression would end in mass killings.

Not all candidates accepted a position in the Judenrat. Some were wise enough to realize that as tempting as this position of privilege was, it would inevitably lead to collaboration in Nazi plans. Samuel Rothenberg, a much-respected pre-war director of the Galicia Oil Refinery, the biggest industrial company in Drohobycz, was one such dissenter. He understood the wisdom of avoiding such a temptation, but there was no lack of willing contenders for his vacancy on the Council.

What were the tempting perks for a member of the Judenrat? Power, of course, better food rations, maybe, but by far, the most important was the assurance of safety for himself and his family. Up to that fateful resettlement day, no one in the Judenrat could have really known what the Nazis had up their sleeve for their Final Solution. One could have even hoped that by skillful cooperation with the Nazis, one could save Jewish lives. But after December, that all changed.

We have all listened with horror to the favorite trick of the Nazis, fictionalized in *Sophie's Choice* [4] but nonetheless based on the oft-repeated fact: "Woman, choose one of your children to be shot, otherwise all of your children will die." We have all considered this as a horrible example of Nazi sadism. It was a no-win situation. What should the stricken woman have done?

If the definition of a sadist is one who inflicts pain to experience pleasure, then this was not the Nazi objective. For Nazis, inflicting pain and death was a matter of policy, a matter of following an order, and a matter of duty. The Nazi atrocity was not about sadism; it was about the physical and moral destruction of a population to be liquidated. The Nazis relied on the fact that a vast majority of mothers would indeed select one child and this in turn would destroy them morally, making them more pliable to Nazi manipulation. Was the woman who selected her child for death a traitor or a victim? Clearly a victim. Was she demoralized? Yes, completely.

This story has an important parallel to the moral trap that the Nazis created for the Judenrat in Drohobycz, in December: "Deliver one thousand Jews in 24 hours or else." The Judenrat delivered them and among the victims of this resettlement to death, was my best friend Benjamin Herbst. Hundreds of Judenrats in Poland received similar Nazi orders, and as the Nazis calculated, the Judenrat delivered their brethren. They chose to collaborate. Just like the mother who gave up her weakest child, they too were victims, demoralized victims.

In December, the Judenrat crossed a moral divide. Decent, normal human beings were now conditioned by this selection to collaborate in more and more gruesome Nazi war crimes. The twelfth century Jewish sage Maimonides (RamBam) who codified the Jewish religious law representing orthodox Judaism to this day, declared: "If pagans should tell you: 'Give us one of yours and we shall kill him, otherwise we shall kill all of you', choose for all to be killed and do not deliver a single Jewish soul." The chief rabbi who sat on the Judenrat in our town did not heed the old sage.

After the December events, the Jewish leadership both locally and worldwide should have shouted: "Your life is not worth anything unless you make it count. Disperse, resist as well as you can. Run away, hide, and fight back. This is your best salvation; this is your only salvation." There undoubtedly would have been severe reprisals, many Jews would have been killed, but the logistics of the extermination of six million people would have been seriously disrupted and disabled. Yet, there was no call for disobedience and resistance, no call to sabotage Heydrich's plan. No Jewish Churchill emerged to lead the fight.

After December, the pressure for the Judenrat to compromise increased. The guarantee of safety for Judenrat members and their families became priceless. Fear corrupts. The power to decide who goes on the next resettlement list and dies and who stays and lives was staggering. Power corrupts.

The Nazi handlers of the Judenrat reasoned: "the quota comes from Berlin. You have no choice. You have the privilege to protect the most worthwhile members of your community. Use it." The distinction between betrayal and protection of the community faded. The realization that the Judenrat had the power to decide on matters of individual life and death motivated those who could afford it, to bribe the right members. The frantic trade to get on a safe list corrupted the whole community. The Judenrat gave donors a temporary and eventually worthless sense of security. The Judenrat became the expeditor and pacifier of the Final Solution.

In March, 1942, another quota for 1,000 Jews was filled. Nine days after Marek and I left Drohobycz, 3,000 more Jews were rounded up in another Action. In October, the Nazis enclosed the Drohobycz ghetto with barbed wire. In November, Sophie and Blima were killed in an "Action on Women" where the Judenrat police were called on to prove their continued loyalty to the Nazis by delivering no less than 100 women per day until a quota of 1,200 women was reached. Some delivered their own mothers.

A year later, the Ukrainian Blackshirts surrounded these same Judenrat policemen on what was left of the Jewish cemetery. Their

German Commander delivered a farewell speech: "I promised that if you followed my orders you would not be deported. I will keep my word; you will be shot right here and now."[12] When the Judenrat's usefulness ended, their collaboration didn't even save their own lives. Only a few survived by hiding.

Heydrich's success in the Jewish annihilation campaign was rewarded by giving him the job of Nazi Governor of the Czechs. Possibly, the ultimate complement to Heydrich's importance was paid by Allied Intelligence. He was the only high-ranking Nazi assassinated during the war: Czech operatives trained by the British MI-5 parachuted into Czechoslovakia in June, 1942, and in a shootout in Prague, fatally injured Heydrich.

Of course, while in the ghetto, I had no knowledge of Reinhard Heydrich or his plan. But without someone on the local level to implement it, Heydrich's plan was just a piece of paper, a report, a presentation. The plan required training gruesome men to bloody their hands in order to implement a gruesome plan. It required the butchery of humans on a scale never before attempted. How could the Nazis find so many volunteers for such an unspeakable assignment? This question has puzzled humanity for years.

But I knew such an implementer in Drohobycz:; I met him and he was Felix Landau, SS Hauptscharführer of the Gestapo. Felix Landau was the Nazi's Judenrat handler in Drohobycz and the man responsible for implementing the Final Solution there. I enclose portions of Landau's diary [5] to see what he had to say about this time period when we both lived there.

In the way of background, Felix Landau was born in Vienna in 1910 to an Austrian mother. His father's name was Stipkowicz, which could imply Polish heritage. Landau was illegitimate. His last name, Landau, came from his stepfather, a Viennese Jew who married his mother and adopted him. In 1931, Landau joined the Nazi party in Vienna at 21 and became an underground member of the SS, the Nazi storm troopers. To say that Landau was a Nazi "from way back" puts it mildly. He joined the Nazis two years before Hitler came to power in Germany.

With the outbreak of the war in 1939, Landau was assigned to Radom in German-occupied Poland. He remained there until 1941, when he volunteered for Einsatz Kommando (EK) duty. EK literally translates as Insertion Command. These paramilitary squads were the Nazi tools for annihilation of Jews and other "undesirables."

Landau recorded his trip from Radom to Lvov and his early stay in Drohobycz in a diary. Years later, when Landau was finally caught and tried in Stuttgart, Germany for war crimes, a certified transcript of the diary was submitted in evidence against him. His murderous acts described in the diary contributed to his 1962 verdict of life in prison. Written in German, the diary covers a period of 3 months and fills 20 typewritten pages in the court-certified transcript. The main theme is a pathetically sentimental moaning about Landau's, a married man, longing for his 21 year old paramour, Gertrude Segel, a typist he had met in Radom. The record of his murderous acts is just interspaced. The abrupt end of the diary may well coincide with Gertrude's transfer to Drohobycz. Landau married Gertrude in 1942, but she divorced Landau after the war.

The diary contains some gems of the career and mentality of an SS man, the "General of the Jews," as he calls himself in his diary. As I translate his diary, I have the feeling that the two of us are looking with hate in each other's eye through opposite ends of a long historical telescope.

Landau comes first to Lvov, the nearest big town to Drohobycz, and joins an Einsatz squad there between July 2 and July 6, where he spends four days busily executing civilians. His duties in Lvov seem like a boot camp for executioners. It would appear that before being entrusted with responsibilities in the Heydrich organization, a member has to have the blood of innocents on his hands. This is a clever way to condemn each to the war criminal status with no way out. A total of 5,000 Jews are killed. In Landau's squad, by his own

Felix Landau (arrow),
Member of the Einsatz Kommando,
arrived in Drohobycz in July 1941

count, contributes more than 800 shot. This is how Felix Landau, with his bloody Nazi credentials and intimate knowledge of Jews, is put in charge of Jewish affairs in Drohobycz and becomes our scourge. Here Landau's beatings and murder are not of the mass variety, as was the case in Lvov, but he still indulges in it to terrorize the population and to keep himself "in shape.

His first notes from Drohobycz shed some interesting light on his instructions on how to form the Judenrat by contacting the "Jewish cultural leader":

July 7, 1941 Today, we have another surprise. A letter from the town military commander arrived in the morning. In an unfriendly tone, we were informed to restrict our activity to censorship of letters. Furthermore we were told to ask no questions from the Jewish cultural leader. As anticipated, this is an impossible relationship. There is a lot of work to do. ---

I was officially appointed as the "General of the Jews." I have again requisitioned two military vehicles for the department. Others have already done that for their own use. I have no time for that. I also only want a decent apartment. The squabbling with the army continues. The major should be considered an enemy of the state. I explained to Berlin that I propose an immediate protective custody be applied against this Major because of his subversive behavior. Especially with regard to his statement that the Jews stand under the protection of the German armed forces. Whoever would have considered something like that possible? He is no Nazi.

There were only sixty-two Gestapo members in Drohobycz, and 15,000 Jews, clearly not enough for what the Germans had in mind. As the General of the Jews, Landau's main responsibility was lining up local manpower for what was then a very secret objective. Landau therefore does not say much in his diary about his responsibility for organizing and supervising the Judenrat. He just mentions a few meetings with them. He talks more about his training of the Ukrainian Blackshirts that will be used extensively in the final liquidation of the Ghetto.

With a feeling of pride, Landau described in detail his participation in the murder of Jews. In his own words:

"*July 11 -12:*

"*In the evening, at 11 o'clock, we came back to the department. Intense activity was going on below in the cellar that I had just emptied of prisoners the previous morning. Fifty prisoners stood there, among them two women. I immediately and voluntarily replaced the man on watch. Almost all prisoners were shot the next day. Among the Jews, most were from Vienna. They still dream about Vienna. My watch lasts until 3 a.m. the next morning. I am dead tired and finally at 3:30 a.m. go to bed.*

"*At 6 o'clock, I am awakened suddenly from solid sleep. Join an execution. Fine, I will act as hangmen and afterwards as gravedigger, why not? It follows that if one loves the fight, then one must shoot up a pile of defenseless people. Twenty-three prisoners are to be shot, the already mentioned women are among them. They can be marveled at. They refuse to take even a glassful of water from us. I am assigned as a guard and I am supposed to shoot anyone trying to escape.*

"*We drive one kilometer along a country road and make a right turn into a forest. At the moment, the detail consists only of six men and we look for a suitable place to shoot and bury the prisoners. After a few minutes we have found a suitable spot. The prisoners to be shot begin to shovel their own graves. Among all of them only two cry. The others have definitely an astonishing courage. What can go on in their heads now? I believe that everyone has a little hope somehow not to be shot. The prisoners work in three shifts because of the number of shovels that we have.*

"*It is peculiar that I am not at all moved. No pity, nothing. It is just so, and all is settled. My heart beats quietly when uncalled-for feelings and thoughts come to me from when I was in a similar situation: On July 24, 1934, in the Chancellor's office, in front of the machine gun fire of the Austrian Army. Then, there have also been moments, when I wanted to become soft, not externally, because that would never be possible with my personality. I was so young and now it is all over. These were thoughts, then I repressed this feeling and in its place came defiance and the realization that my death would not have been in vain.*

"*Now, I stand today as a survivor in front of others, about to shoot them. Slowly the pit becomes bigger and bigger. The two cry continuously. I let them dig a longer grave, so that they don't think so much. While laboring they are actually calmer. All valuables, watches and money are put together in a pile. Afterwards the prisoners are all brought side by side in an open place. The two women were shot first at one end of the grave. Two men were already shot in the bushes by (our auxiliaries). I have not seen this because I had to keep an eye on the other prisoners. The bodies of women were thrown forward by the shots, spun around, and came to rest next to the pit.*

"My partner and I had to shoot six men. We divided the targets, three men in the heart; three men in the head. I chose the heart. We started shooting and pieces of brain whizzed through the air. Two shots to the head are too much. You almost tear the head off. Almost all bodies sank silently together. Only with two it didn't work out, they howled and whimpered for a long time. The shots from a revolver were of no use. The two of us who shot together have no misses.

"The next-to-last group of prisoners must now throw those already shot into the mass grave and then in turn, line up to be shot and fall into the grave. The last two prisoners are forced to sit on the forward edge of the grave so that they fall right inside. Only, some corpses still have to be moved around with a pick, and then we begin with the job of covering the graves.

"July 22: The day is eventful. In the morning, the workers that I ordered arrived.

Just as I wanted to go to the Judenrat, one of the workers came and requested my support since the Jews refused to work here. I went over. As these assholes saw me, they all scattered in different directions. It is a shame I did not have a pistol with me, because I would have shot some into a pile. I now went to the Judenrat and told them that if 100 Jews don't line up in an hour, I will pick out myself 100 Jews, but not for work but to be shot.

Hardly 30 minutes later, 100 Jews arrived and furthermore an additional 17 men in place of the ones that had escaped first. I reported the incident and demanded at the same time that the escapees must be shot for refusing to work. That happened exactly 12 hours later, 20 Jews were killed . . ."

This incident happened just around the corner from our apartment on Mickiewicz Street, as we were packing to leave. When I came home from work that night, Tova was even more nervous than usual and told me about the events of the day. A group of 17 Jews at the *Sicherheitpolizei* (Security Police) building site ran away because of beatings. Three of them hid in our house for a few hours. Their Jewish foreman reported the escape to Landau.

When the workday had ended, the replacement 117 Jews who carried bricks for construction were released. Landau and his cronies randomly rounded up 20 Jews, lined them up at attention for about an hour at the work site, and then Landau personally killed every second one in the row and released the ten survivors. Landau was not interested in identifying or punishing the actual 17 escapees.

"July 28: Ukrainians found 24 Ukrainians murdered by the Russians in the forest. The corpses are almost unrecognizable. The Kripo (German Criminal Police) officials consider it a murder and drive to this place. There, they are solemnly received by a priest and are cordially greeted. The priest thinks it is unusually kind that the Germans take so much interest in the assassination and in the fate of the Ukrainians. The corpses are buried solemnly and our officials take part in the ceremony. On the way the priest explains to me, 'Do you know the most wicked deed is that someone has put Jewish passports and papers into the pockets of the Ukrainians?' Now that rings the bell. These supposedly murdered Ukrainians were the 23 Jews and I believe 2 Ukrainians (apparently an error in addition by Landau), that we shot under martial law. The documents of the dead already stank awfully. I let them be soaked with gasoline, burnt and buried in the pit.

"August 1: The G.G. (abbreviation unknown, probably a commanding officer) should come tomorrow and my militia must be clothed. I came in the evening at 7 p.m. into their barracks and find out that of the 60 men, only 12 were clothed. For almost three days, approximately 40 (Jewish) tailors worked and could not finish it. Now, however, I became wild. To a large extent, of course, the blame rested with the militia leadership. I let the Judenrat immediately come to me and I explained that all lacking uniforms must be ready by noon tomorrow, otherwise I will shoot 5 tailors because of sabotage.

"August 2: The G.G doesn't come. At 12 o'clock, the Judenrat elder reported to me that all uniforms were ready. In spite of this, I had 20 men shot for dragging their feet.

"August 13: Jewish apartment house is evacuated and tomorrow the work begins anew."

This is the apartment house where I lived.

The last entry in the diary comes on October 2, 1941. Very likely, Gertrude joined Landau soon after and his motivation to talk to her through his diary vanished.

After the war, Landau was declared a war criminal. In 1947 he escaped the American POW camp in Glassenbach. Landau lived under a false identity for 12 years but was recognized and arrested in Stuttgart, Germany in 1959. His diary was presented at his trials as part of the evidence against him. A Stuttgart court sentenced Landau to life in prison in 1962.

The Nazis organized and cajoled the Jews in hundreds of towns like ours by the same methods. The Judenrat's collaboration pacified millions of Jews and helped the Nazis to demoralize, segregate, and isolate them into ghettos that became trans-shipment points to crematoria. The perfidy of Heydrich's plan, and its implementation by Landau in Drohobycz, was that it required little German manpower and resources. The annihilation cost Germany little and produced substantial benefits from Jewish slave labor. All Jewish properties were confiscated, right down to the gold in their teeth and the hair from their heads.

The question of the role of the Judenrat in the Holocaust has tortured me for a long time. The pain of this memory has been the reason why, for 50 years, I have not willingly talked about my World War II experiences. I could not disassociate my story from recollections of Judenrat actions. Yet to speak of the Judenrat as Nazi collaborators always felt to me like a desecration of a Holocaust cemetery.

Clearly, it is easier and more charitable to simply consider the Judenrat as victims rather than traitors who were double-crossed by their handlers. Many survivors of the Holocaust undoubtedly share these feelings. Yet, when I think of the death of my friend Benjamin Herbst, I feel I have an obligation to write down my memories and share my thoughts, as I agonize to understand how it could have happened. Now people say: "Never again." I have to ask: "Why in the first place?" I had to understand from a historical perspective why there was so much collaboration and so little opposition?

It is most important that my thoughts are not misinterpreted:

I do not mean to imply that if it were not for the Judenrat, there would have been no Holocaust. The Judenrat was only one cog in the vast machinery of extermination. In some places, like the occupied Soviet territories, Judenrats were never formed. Nazi murder squads followed combat troops into occupied territory and murdered Jews on the spot.

Also, I do not mean in any way to imply a moral flaw in the victims of the Holocaust. Within years of the end of the war, survivors of the ghetto risked their lives without hesitation, fighting for the independence of Israel, but courage needs leadership and inspiration to risk all. Our tragedy was that in the ghetto, we had neither.

Whether or not historians will accept or even consider my explanation, only time will tell, but my understanding of Heydrich's trap has helped me quiet my ghosts. Without the need for whitewash or obfuscation, without twisting the exception and the rule of the Judenrat operation, I can now face my memories of this most tragic page in Jewish history.

Chapter 7

My Teachers

I cannot end the recollections of my life in Drohobycz without paying respect to my high school teachers. Secondary education in Poland was not compulsory. In the nineteen thirties, the Polish public high schools and academic institutions adopted a quota system severely limiting the enrolment of Jews. As a defensive measure, the Jewish community in Drohobycz organized a private high school named after Leon Sternbach, a local academic and historian. A well respected teacher Jacob Blatt, formerly from the state high school, became the principal. The school was typically referred to as Blatt's Gimnazjum. Both the student body and the faculty were Jewish although the curriculum was that of a strictly Polish high school. As these were depression years, there was a huge pool of unemployed Jewish intellectuals with prestigious advanced degrees for selection to the faculty. The intellect and qualifications of our faculty rivaled today's best universities. Blatt's Gimnazjum had a lasting influence on my life.

One of my teachers is now the greatly admired writer and painter, Bruno Schulz. His writing has inspired a generation of authors in Europe, the United States, and even in Japan. Some consider him the new prophet of Israel. His literary talents were beginning to be appreciated in pre-war Polish literary circles, but in
my high school days, he certainly was not recognized as the genius that he was by his students or the local town's people. We saw him

as a frail, sickly, and sad-looking high school teacher, pushing fifty, who taught drawing, drafting, and shop in the State High School.

My first recollection of Professor Schulz was when I was fourteen. In 1939, just before the war, he caused a minor scandal in our town by officially resigning from the Jewish religious community. This was generally the first step in converting to another religion. Membership in a religious community was a compulsory part of the legal structure of society in Poland since the religious community handled and recorded births, marriages, and deaths.

Like my father, Bruno Schulz was an assimilated Jew who spoke and wrote in Polish and, short of possibly attending a synagogue on high holidays, cared little about religious rituals. Still, his resignation from the Jewish religious community was a drastic step that caused a lot of gossip. Speculation was that he did it to marry Josefina Szelinska, his fiancée of several years, who was herself a Jewish convert to Catholicism and, at one time, his colleague teacher at the high school. The marriage never took place.

Before the war, Bruno Schulz taught shop and drawing in the state high school *Panstwowe Gimnazjum* in Drohobycz. In 1939, the curriculum changed to the Soviet system and the transition was a mess. Since it did not include shop, Schulz's class was eliminated and he had to look for other opportunities. The principal of our formerly private high school, Jacob Blatt, was one of the few people in our town that had some inkling of Schulz's extraordinary talents and arranged for him to teach literature in his school during the school year 1939-40. Our class was a temporary expediency, but it was probably the only time that this genius of literature actually taught this subject. This is how Bruno Schulz became my Literature teacher at Blatt's Gimnazjum.

**Below is a graduation photo of the Class of 1940
in my high school
(Photo courtesy of my friend George Oscar Lee)**

Bruno Schulz is on the extreme left, looking down. To the right is Professor Ohrenstein, my math teacher. The woman with flowers and the man with glasses to the right are the Landmans. She taught languages; he taught physics. On the lower right with the mustache is Professor Jacob Blatt, Principal of the school. The pre-war name of the school was Leon Sternbach Gimnazjum but it was usually referred to as Blatt's Gimnazjum. Top left is the ever present picture of Stalin. To the left of it and respectfully lower is a picture of Karl Marx. None of the above faculty survived the Holocaust. The Landmans committed suicide a few weeks after the Nazi invasion. Jacob Blatt walked naked to his grave[12] in the woods of Bronica quoting Immanuel Kant. I wonder if it was: "For if justice and righteousness perish, human life would no longer have any value in the world."

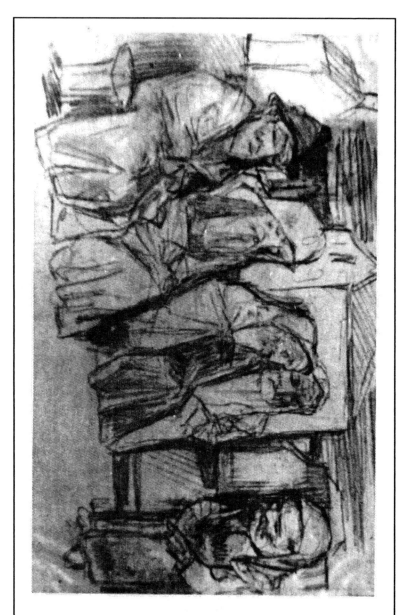

Waiting for the Messiah
(A drawing by Bruno Schulz)

Professor Schulz was a very mild man who had problems keeping discipline in class even under the best circumstances. One dark wintry evening the electricity failed in our school, a fairly common problem under the Soviets. In the darkness, all hell broke loose. Professor Schulz softly began to tell a story in an even, melodic voice. Row by row, the class quieted down, first listening, then becoming engrossed, and then finally entranced by his tale. Just listening to Bruno Schulz was mesmerizing, absorbing, dream like. One could hear a pin drop. When the lights came back, we remained still, looking with some embarrassment at each other. He had reached the child in us. Bruno Schulz never had any disrespect in our class again. In that darkness, his artistic soul made magic contact with ours and we loved it. We secretly hoped for more blackouts with Bruno Schulz.

Under the Nazis, the definition of Jew was based on hereditary rather than religious background. Although Schulz had resigned from the Jewish religious community, Schulz was a Jew again when the Germans occupied Drohobycz in 1941. SS Hauptscharführer Felix Landau, the Nazi butcher of Drohobycz, demanded that the Labor Office supply someone to decorate Nazi buildings and residences. The Judenrat assigned Bruno Schulz to serve as the artist.

The strange paradox of human nature is that Felix Landau had an artistic spark in his black soul and recognized the artistic quality of Schulz. Schulz became a slave protégé of Landau. On orders, Shultz painted Landau's portrait. He painted murals and other artwork in Nazi halls. He even painted fairy tale figures on the nursery walls of Landau's house. Sadly, even Landau's patronage of Schulz did not save him. On November 19, 1942, another Nazi shot Schulz in the street as retribution against Landau.

After more than a half century, the murals that Schulz painted on the walls of Landau's son's nursery in Drohobycz were the subject of a bitter international dispute. In 2001, workers from Yad Vashim, Israel's Holocaust Museum, chiseled five fragments from the fairy tale murals in Drohobycz and took them to Israel for restoration and placement in the new museum. This prompted a dispute with the Ukrainians and Poles concerning the legality of removing the relics. [6]

I often tried to recall the subject matter of Schulz's enchanting stories in that darkened classroom. I never knew if he was reciting from his own work or if he was quoting from others. One seemingly meaningless and strange detail has stuck in my memory all of these years, the mention of a messiah from Sambor. I remember it because coincidentally, I was born in Sambor, a small town some thirty miles west of Drohobycz. It turns out that this was an important clue.

Under Soviet occupation, Schulz continued working on his last book, the *Messiah*. As he feared for his life under the Nazis, Schulz gave the manuscript for safekeeping to a non-Jewish friend, but the manuscript vanished during the war. In 1986, there was some hope that the manuscript had been found. Nothing came of this except a fictional novel by Cynthia Ozick entitled *The Messiah of Stockholm*.

Only the opening line of Schulz's *Messiah* was preserved in the memory of his friend.[7] The line was typical Bruno Schulz whimsy: *"You know - my mother said this morning - the Messiah has arrived. He is already in Sambor."* We can only hope that a bunch of unruly high school students during a blackout is not going to be the last audience to hear the messiah story of the good genius of Drohobycz.

Part 2

Go East, Young Man

Chapter 8

Escape to Lvov

Janek's horse-drawn wagon was headed for Stryi, a neighboring town some thirty miles away. Marek and I tried to "relax" as we traveled along a bumpy, dirt road going through fields of wheat and potatoes. Here and there I could see children playing near thatched peasant huts with small windows. Typically, a small barn stood next to the hut. Occasionally, the strong smell of an open septic pond that collected natural fertilizers from the outhouse and the barn animals wafted through the air. Still, it was wonderful to ride in the open, without the stigma of the Star of David armband. Janek pulled out a bottle of homemade vodka and passed the bottle around. Marek and I took a polite gulp. Janek indulged with gusto. It did not matter much if Janek was drunk; the horse knew the way. We all broke into a Polish song about the ample anatomy of a girl named Manka and we proceeded on our way as if we did not have a care in the world. I would now start a new life as Leslaw Strutinski.

Marek and I stayed for the night in the barn of Janek's farmer friend and we slept in the straw. In the morning, Janek unloaded shoes and clothing that he had acquired the day before in Drohobycz and loaded various food items destined for trading at the next stop. After an early breakfast of bread as dark as rich soil and a glass of warm milk straight from the cow, we proceeded towards our objective, Lvov, another 60 miles away. Late in the afternoon, tired and dirty, we arrived at a trolley terminal on the outskirts of Lvov. We bid our farewells to Janek as he continued on to sell his hams, chickens, and honey on Lvov's black market. Marek and I dusted off

My Father in 1938

and hopped onto a trolley car headed for the city.

This trip was quite different from my first visit. Once before the war, when I was eleven, my father took me on an exciting trip to Lvov. It was just the two of us. We traveled in a first-class compartment with upholstered furniture, and lace curtains on the windows. My father had a contract with the Polish Railways

to provide dental services to railroad employees and free first class travel was one of the perks. My father enjoyed introducing me to new experiences and beautiful places and Lvov was such a place. It was a bustling metropolis with stunningly tall and beautiful buildings. The architecture was mostly a legacy of the two centuries before World War I, when Lvov was the capital of the Austrian Eastern Galicia Province. Lvov is where I first saw trolley cars. My father took me out to lunch and we had big sandwiches with wonderful cheese. In the evening, he took me to the opera house where I saw

Madama Butterfly. I was a bit overwhelmed by the music but the moving scenery fascinated me.

But on this day in August, 1942, I was no longer surrounded by beauty nor was I happily traveling with my father holding my hand. The city now looked much shabbier and I was fully preoccupied with worries about a new life under an assumed identity. The trolley car was packed with people returning home from work. I expected that at any minute, we would be stopped by a policeman and unmasked, but no one paid us any attention. We headed for Lvov because it was a large city where no one would know us and where it should be easier to blend. As a transportation hub, it also seemed like a logical launching point for our vague pipe dreams of eventually escaping the German occupation and joining the allies.

The real Leslaw Strutinski had given me the address of a Polish Catholic woman with whom we could stay for a couple of days. It was early evening when we found her place. We were not quite sure what she knew about our true identity. The woman's name was Anna. She was in her fifties and she lived in a small apartment filled with rather elegant furniture. She greeted us warmly, said that she had a postcard about our visit from her cousin in Drohobycz, and offered us some food. After dinner, she told us that she was a nanny to a Lvov Jewish family for most of her life and she had felt like a part of that family. The family was moved to the Janowska Street camp some weeks before our arrival, then they were shipped to a death camp. She thought the Jewish family was wonderful and she mourned their loss as genuinely as if they were her own. Did she know that we were Jewish escapees from the ghetto? If so, she risked her life for strangers, not for money but out of true compassion. She satisfies my requirements for sainthood and remains as such in my memory.

In the evening at Anna's, we looked for rooms to rent in the local Polish paper and we selected a few likely prospects. For safety reasons, Marek and I decided to proceed separately from now on. This way, if one of us got caught, the other would not be arrested. The next day, I would look for a permanent address. There were two key steps necessary to establish my new identity. I needed a work card and an identity card showing registration with the police. An explanation of my background was necessary for this registration. Movement from one town to another without authorization was not allowed. My explanation would be that I was a Polish deportee, shipped with my family by the Soviets to Kazakhstan. I recently escaped from the USSR and so it was my first registration. I had no idea how carefully anyone would scrutinize my story.

The next morning I found a room (more of an oversized closet) with a Polish working class family. Of course, they rented the room to Leslaw Strutinski and knew nothing of my background. I had to assure them that I would have the required police registration before I moved in. Next, I went to the Work Office. It was a big operation run by the Germans with mostly local clerical help. I practiced my story over and over in my head. There were long lines of people being slowly processed at cubicle windows. The man ahead of me reported that his job was complete and he asked for a new assignment. I was given a form to fill out and sent to another line at another window where new work documents were issued. I completed the form, giving my occupation as electrician's helper. The clerk who processed my form was a young Polish woman who fortunately was not in the mood to ask me too many questions. She filled in my work document and left it on the desk of her German boss to sign. He was not there and it took him another ten minutes to return. It was a very long ten minutes for me. He signed three work documents that were on his desk and left again. In a few minutes, the clerk called: "Leslaw Strutinski." My heart leaped with joy when I saw that she had my signed work document. I went back to another window and got my work assignment for the next morning on a construction site.

In the afternoon, I decided to climb the next hurdle and register with the police. The Germans also ran the Police Station, again with local help in lower clerical positions. Being discovered by the police was not the only danger. We were warned that the *szmalcownicy* (the Polish name for local blackmailers that were good at recognizing well-off Jews using a false identity) hung out near registration places, ready to extort new victims. At the police station, I filled out another form and enclosed with it my treasured birth certificate of Leslaw Strutinski. After a while, I was given a temporary ID card and registration and one week's worth of food ration coupons. I was told to come back in a week to pick up the permanent papers. I was 17 and I had a new name, address, and job.

Marek and I met at Anna's late the next afternoon. He was also successful in getting settled. He obtained a job in a warehouse and a place to stay. We were both elated at having survived the day although we still feared problems concerning the permanent ID papers. We profusely thanked Anna and moved out to our new places. After a week, we both got our permanent police registration and our food ration coupons. I received my birth certificate back. Leslaw and Marek had sprouted roots in Lvov. It worked!

On my job, I wired electric power lines for a German office building. Since my childhood, I had been fascinated with electricity and so I found the job interesting and I was learning a lot. I gave my landlady my ration book and made arrangements with her for room and board. The food rations depended on ethnicity: 2,614 calories per day for Germans, 669 calories for Poles, and 184 calories for Jews. As mentioned, rations for the Jews were completely inadequate for survival without some sort of black market barter. Food rations for the non-Jewish local population were above the starvation level but left us constantly hungry. If a Pole or Ukrainian wanted to claim German ancestry, however loosely, he could become a *Volksdeutsche* (ethnic German) and his rations were much better. On top of the feeding chain were the *Reichsdeutsche* (Germans born in the Reich). They had special stores and practically no restriction on the amount of food. All of the best restaurants in town were marked *Nur Fur Reichsdeutsche* (For-Reich-Germans-Only) and they showed menus that were comparable to pre-war fare. No food coupons were required.

Once in a while at night, hunger would wake me. I would sneak into the kitchen and cut off a thin slice of bread, hoping that the landlady would not notice it in the morning. I was deeply ashamed of stealing food from others who would then be even hungrier. Yet persistent hunger is a powerful motivator. Finally, I decided to supplement my diet in a much more dangerous but also more moral and fulfilling way. On Sunday, my day off, I wore my best clothes, polished my shoes, and walked to the For-Reich-Germans-Only restaurant. I had spent some time "casing" the place. The Germans were not asked for identification. It seemed that speaking German, swagger, and arrogance to local waiters were all that was required for entry. I had a good ear for languages since German was a second language at my home. (My father had attended medical school in Vienna where he met and married my mother and so they both spoke fluent German.) Also, my age did not seem to be a problem since Germans who were my age and dressed in civilian clothes frequented the restaurant. Inwardly, I pumped myself up with Germanic importance, made some brusque remarks to the waiter who led me to the table, and I brazenly ordered sauerbraten with potato pancakes. The food was delicious and plentiful. The meal was definitely worth getting shot for.

The Sunday dinner became a tradition and I was getting better and more comfortable as a Reich German. I realized that I was getting good at playing this role, and the role was reasonably safe because the chances of Germans being asked for identification were quite small. Awareness of this security loophole later proved to have a far greater survival value than the extra calories (as wonderful as they were at the time).

One day, while riding back from work on the trolley, two Gestapo men jumped onto the trolley: one through the front entrance and the other through the back. They were checking ID papers and scrutinizing the passengers. I handed over my papers and froze: the Gestapo man looked at the papers, looked me over, and moved on. What a relief! Farther down the trolley, there was a commotion. The Gestapo held a Jewish-looking man and woman. They dragged them from the trolley. Jews had been escaping from Lvov's Ghetto and the Gestapo dragnets for the escapees were getting more frequent. Marek experienced several such checks that he also managed to survive. How long would our luck in Lvov last? One day, I showed Marek a curious ad that I found in the classified section of the local Polish newspaper: "Experienced construction workers and draftsmen wanted in Kiev (Ukraine). Good pay and food rations. Other benefits. Call xxxxxx." Getting out of Lvov would be great yet the ad seemed highly suspicious. It was obviously an odd deal. We decided that it was likely to be some sort of a trap.

A week later I went to the movies on Saturday night. I saw a German film, pretty boring at that, but it was the only Saturday night entertainment available. The movie house was crowded and the exit door was narrow. It took quite a few minutes to push my way out after the movie. At the trolley stop, I reached for my wallet to get the right change for the fare. My wallet was gone! Someone had picked my pockets. There was not much money in it but all of my carefully collected ID papers were gone.

The gruesome reality struck like lightning; there was no way that I could regain the lost documents. I still had my birth certificate at home but having this as the only proof of my identity was flaky enough the first time around. I could never survive the scrutiny of reporting my papers lost. Without papers, I would be picked up on the next ID check. Without money for the trolley fare, I glumly walked home. After a while, the numb despair started to lift. I remembered the Kiev ad and wondered if this could be a way out?

The next morning, Sunday, I called the number in the ad. It was clearly a private number since I could hear a crying child in the background. A man by the name of Romek gave me his address and I arranged to meet him. Romek was a Pole in his early twenties. He explained the deal: He worked for a German construction firm named Kurt Wuttge that had a construction contract with the German Railroads. They were part of the paramilitary Organization Todt (named after Fritz Todt, Germany's armaments minister). The firm was desperately short of construction foremen, carpenters, and draftsmen and they were way behind in their schedule. The boss sent Romek to Lvov to do some clandestine recruiting, clandestine because the Lvov German authorities did not approve it. However, Romek had official German Railroad travel orders. So, once we were on the train, we would be all right. Our presence in Kiev would be fully sanctioned due to the firm's connections and their high priority work assignment.

This sounded better than I expected. I told Romek that I was interested in the draftsman job. He said that I would need to know German and Russian to be able to translate drawings in their Kiev office. "I am your man," I assured Romek. Indeed, I had a fair knowledge of German and I had two years of Russian in high school (under the 1939-41 Soviet occupation) which also would come in handy. The couple of hours of drafting classes that I had in school were a stretch, but I was sure that I could wing it. I also exaggerated my newly acquired electrician's experience. "Can you translate construction details from German into Russian?" Romek tested in heavily accented German. "Yes, I can do that and I can do drafting," I answered, also in German. He asked me to write a couple of sentences in Russian. I did it. Romek did not require a lot of arm-twisting since the firm really needed a draftsman/translator and, in any case, his reward was a per-head bounty.

"I can fit you into the transport that leaves in two weeks," he said. *Anything leaving sooner?* I asked. Romek smiled. He rightly suspected that I had a really hot problem on my hands. "Well, I have a transport leaving at 7 p.m. this evening. The list is closed but I guess I can fit you in."

"Suits me; I will be there" I assured him. I worried about documents. "Do I need to bring along *anything?*" "No Leslaw," Romek said, now comprehending my problem, "you will be covered by the Military Travel Order. Just be there at 7 p.m. in front of the newspaper kiosk." "*Danke, dzienkuje, spasiba,*" I said, thanking him in German, Polish, and Russian and running out.

I was elated. All I needed now was to survive without documents between 11 a.m. and 7 p.m. I went to see Marek. He was as excited as I was about the Kiev connection. "This sounds great. When you get to Kiev, write me. If it is as good as it sounds, I will join you." I collected my belongings, which easily fit into a small suitcase. I told my landlady that my mother was seriously ill and I would have to be with her for a while. She was very happy that I left her my food coupons for the next two weeks. I saw it as overdue compensation for those midnight raids into the kitchen for bread slices.

I was at the railroad station at 6 p.m. and walked back and forth along the street and watched the newspaper kiosk in front of the railroad station. I did not approach the kiosk until a few minutes before the specified 7 p.m. hour. A group of about 20 men gathered there. Their ages ranged from late teens to maybe thirty. They spoke Polish. It was pretty clear that most were quite nervous. It was obvious this was not a group looking for career opportunities and a nice trip to the Ukraine. They were looking for an escape. I scrutinized their faces trying to figure out why. A few faces looked possibly Jewish; a few might have been political dissidents; a few of the faces I would not like to meet in a dark ally. Except for neutral comments like "I wonder when Romek will show up," we did not say much to each other. We just waited quietly and nervously.

Then, three burly Poles arrived. "Oh, here is the transport," said one. "See any Kikes?" asked another. They picked one of the Jewish-looking men. "Hey, Jew where do you think you're going?" The man was white as a sheet. "I am not a Jew," he protested. "OK, drop your pants and show me," demanded the tormentor. "What do you want from me?" cried the victim. "Money, money," said the Pole. The victim handed them a bunch of paper notes. "You can keep this," one said "we only accept gold twenties." The victim hesitated, then poked around in the lining of his jacket and produced one U.S. $20 gold piece, the extortionists' standard currency. "Twenty for *each* of us," yelled the blackmailer. "I don't have it," cried the victim. "How much do you have?" "Just one more," he whimpered. "Then, give it to me," the bully shouted. The victim obliged. "Have a good trip, Kike," said the satisfied bullies, laughing as they left.

The transport group watched the episode in stone silence. We were clearly relieved that the "disturbance" was settled quickly and did not attract police attention. Romek showed up and one of the group whispered something into his ear. Romek walked over to the victim. "You are not going with us. You will endanger the whole transport." The victim visibly shook. We nervously followed Romek into the station. Our train had a big slogan painted on it: *Rader mussen rollen fur dem Sieg* (Wheels must roll for victory). "Let 'em roll, please God, let us roll right out of here!" I prayed.

Romek found the German train commander and showed him the group's papers. The train was full of German troops. Our group was assigned to a corner of a freight car that was almost full of boxes and packages of various types. I heard the whistle and much to my relief the train rolled out of Lvov.

Chapter 9

Kiev Disaster

Lvov and Kiev, though both occupied by the Germans, were administratively quite different: Lvov was a part of the *Generalgouvernement*, the German name for occupied Polish territories. Kiev, on the other hand was part of the occupied USSR, officially designated *Reichskommissariat fur Ukraine*. A border crossing was still maintained between the two regions at Rovno. In the eyes of the Germans, this border separated European civilization from Soviet barbarism. The situation on each side of the border was quite different. As mentioned earlier, west of the border, Jews were killed in somewhat disguised Nazi gas chambers. East of the border, the Nazi Einsatz Kommando simply shot Jews in front of mass graves. So in 1942, there were still many Jews alive west of the border. East of the border, the Reichskommissariat territory was *Judenfrei* (free of Jews).

Our train reached Rovno in about three hours, on Sunday night at about 10 o'clock. The German border patrol looked through our boxcar. Romek's travel orders sufficed. The patrol looked with some disbelief at our motley group but moved on. Since we were traveling on a German military order for the firm of Kurt Wuttge, the railroad contractor, we were allowed to get some good food at the railway field kitchen. The toilets at the station were also welcome. Our

68

boxcar lacked any such niceties and serious relief required rather acrobatic and risky contortions on the short walk between the railroad cars.

Military trains ran according to priorities and ours did not have a high one. We waited for a couple of hours before the train moved again. This was only the first of many stops on this 350-mile trip from Lvov to Kiev. We did not get to the Kiev railroad station until Monday evening. Since it was getting close to curfew when we arrived, a soldier was assigned to escort us. We marched from the railroad station to the dormitory where we were going to stay. The route went through Khreschatyk, the main thoroughfare of Kiev. On their withdrawal the previous summer, the Soviets had installed disguised, time-delay mines in every building on the street. When the Germans occupied Kiev, they quartered their commands in buildings along Khreschatyk. Three days after the Soviet withdrawal, the bombs detonated, all at the same time, costing the Germans and locals many casualties and Kiev its main street. That night we marched after curfew through a totally deserted Khreschatyk with the bombed-out remainders of walls and chimneys reaching to the moonlit sky, like an eerie gigantic monument to the suffering of the victims of war.

The next day, the construction firm's office processed us and assigned employment. I had my picture taken, and a few days later, I received an official ID card (*Kenncarte*) with all kinds of impressive stamps and the German eagle sitting on top of a swastika. What a relief! I did not feel naked anymore. In general, I felt a lot more secure in Kiev than I did in Lvov. There was no Jewish ghetto, no local escapees, and no need for dragnets so common in Lvov. All local Jews had been shot by the *Einsatz Kommando* in the Babi Yar, a ravine on the outskirts of Kiev, shortly after the German occupation. A Polish Jew in disguise with reasonably Aryan looks was not likely to be recognized, while in Lvov the slightest nuance of expression or body language could be detected by local *szmalcownicy* and used for extortion. As "essential foreign workers", our food rations were better. Relatively inexpensive and easily obtainable black market food was openly traded in bazaars. I was not hungry any more. I wrote to Marek and advised him to come.

A German manager ran the firm with his young German secretary named Gertrude. I was assigned to the Kiev office with three other people from my transport. Two other Lvov natives were already there from an earlier trip. The rest of my group was assigned directly to the construction sites depending on their trades. About a dozen office employees were local, mostly women. My job was to look at the German notations on original drawings and specifications of railway water towers and storage sheds. I translated the German into Russian and entered this information on the detailed drawings and specifications prepared in the office by local draftsmen. In so doing, the local construction crews could understand the notations. Why in Russian? Because Russian, not Ukrainian, was the working language in Kiev.

After receiving my letter, Marek decided to take the plunge and arrived in Kiev early in November. He also got a job in the Kiev office where he tracked the distribution of building materials. We felt safe enough to rent some rooms together. Now I had a few hours every day where I could revert to my true identity. Much to my surprise, it was more difficult than I suspected. Since my life depended on the Leslaw identity, I absorbed it so thoroughly that reverting to Edwin was full of foreboding.

Marek was fascinated with the Lvov-Kiev escape path that we uncovered. He felt that a lot of Jews could be shipped through it out of Lvov. He was getting friendly with Romek and was trying to get involved in the transports. Was he motivated by the desire to help our compatriots? This was undoubtedly important to him, but what really fascinated Marek was the business opportunity. A safe escape from the Ghetto was worth a lot of money. Marek felt that if he made contact with the Ghetto, he could get a thousand gold dollars per escapee. In a few trips, he could make a fortune.

Snow came early to Kiev in 1942 and with it, two strange events that seem at first disconnected. On a snowy Saturday morning early in December, I was walking through the bazaar to do some food shopping when I saw a remarkable sight. A motley group of Italian soldiers was trying to barter their submachine guns for food. Italians were fighting on the side of the Germans and their presence in Kiev would not have been all that surprising but these soldiers were unshaven, dirty, and hungry. Who but a deserter would want to trade his gun for food? A few weeks later, Gertrude, the office secretary, burst out crying in the middle of the office Christmas party and ran out of the room. The German manager explained: "Her fiancée is in Stalingrad. She hasn't heard from him for a while." The German news reported only heavy fighting in Stalingrad. At that time, I had no idea that half of a million soldiers of the German Sixth Army were surrounded, their Romanian and Italian allies destroyed, and that Germany was about to suffer its first devastating defeat of World War II.

Meanwhile, Marek had succeeded in his plans to become a transport leader between Lvov and Kiev. In January, Romek came down with the flu and could not travel. Marek promised to split his black market profit from the trip with Romek, if he recommended him. The black market contraband had nothing to do with transporting Jews. Marek, just like Romek, would buy food in Kiev and sell it in Lvov and then buy manufactured goods like cloth dyes in Lvov and sell them in Kiev, thereby quadrupling their money on the trip. They knew that no one checked for contraband on military trains. On that trip Marek made his contact with the Ghetto and transported one Jew from there. Unlike Romek, who might have transported a Jew inadvertently, Marek knew what he was doing. The fee that he earned made the black market profit seem like small change. Marek doubled his per trip payoff to Romek, and Romek, who was getting tired of all the travel, resigned the job in Marek's favor.

Marek's and my social life became a great success without too much effort on our part. The demographics were to blame. Because of the war, there must have been ten eligible women in Kiev for every eligible man. Condoms were expensive and hard to find, but I managed to get them on the black market. In addition to obvious good reasons for using them, they also covered my circumcision. Marek got carried away and got his Russian girl friend Katia pregnant. After some arm-twisting, he agreed to marry her. It was not just because it was the right thing to do. I think that Marek loved her and he was excited about being a father. What was hard for me to understand, however, was how they could be so close and yet, he kept his being Jewish a secret from her. In March, they had a Greek Orthodox Church wedding including a bearded priest with a booming basso voice. After the ceremony, the newly wed couple spent half an hour together and the mother-in-law produced a bloodstained sheet to prove that the bride was a virgin. What a joke! I was thinking of the plot of *Madama Butterfly* although Marek's good-looking but solidly built bride was no fluttering insect.

Shortly after the wedding, my comfortable life in Kiev ended. My German boss told me that I would be working at the railroad water tower construction near Vinnitsa, about 150 miles southwest of Kiev. It was an emergency because an important military headquarters was located nearby. Soviet partisans blew up the old tower, and the German railroad was having difficulty supplying the water required to run steam locomotives. They now had a German military contingent providing security and supervising the construction, but they needed more hands to work on construction. They picked me because I could also translate between the Germans and the construction crew. Or at least I was told so, to soften the blow of the transfer to manual work. Since this was a field job, I was given a perk, a green uniform with Organization Todt woven into the cuff of the sleeve. Remembering the lesson of the German restaurant dinners in Lvov, I had the uniform custom fitted by a Kiev tailor to make sure that I looked as important as I could muster.

I reported to Gertrude to get my travel papers. She opened a safe in her small office and pulled out a Military Travel Order from a pile of maybe a dozen already stamped and signed documents. I looked at the forms with awe. This piece of paper could get me anywhere. After all, this piece of paper got Romek's transport from Lvov to

Kiev without problems. Powerful stuff. She was also going to give
me some travel money but there was none in the safe. She went to
the boss's office to get some money from the petty cash box. The
safe was open and I quickly grabbed three Travel Order forms while
she was gone. When she got back in a couple of minutes, the Travel
Orders were in my pocket.

I later decided to organize a "First Aid Kit." From the supply
closet, I took a pen like Gertrude used for filling out documents. I
then filled a very small bottle with ink, in case the Germans used
recognizable ink on travel orders and so that the signature and text
ink matched. I bought a couple of rubber erasers, a small bottle of
liquid ink eraser, and a small magnifying glass. I bought two identical
small travel bags and made it into one with a double bottom. In
between the two bottoms, I placed my stolen Travel Order forms,
forging tools, some money, my father's gold watch, and a railroad
map of the Ukraine. Then I carefully slid into the compartment my
grandmother's diary, my Ark of the Covenant that foretold my
survival of the war. I sealed the double bottom. It was a pretty neat
job for an amateur.

The water tower was in the middle of nowhere near a railroad
junction, some 30 miles before Vinnitsa, the nearest train stop. I
traveled there with a Polish foreman who knew the place. He
explained that we had two choices to get there. One choice was to
ride to the train station in Vinnitsa, and try to hitch a ride back along
the road, the 30 miles to the water tower. Considering that it was late
March and the snow had started melting, the road was a hopeless
quagmire of mud. The second choice was to jump from the train
near the tower construction site, to save us the 30-mile trip back. To
him it was a no-brainer: we were going to jump. "That is how my
crew travels and as far as I know, no one has gotten killed" - he told
me with some pride. "How about broken bones?" I asked. He
shrugged his shoulders. He gave me my train-jumping training:
"When the train slows to about 25 mph on a turn that he would
point out, throw your bags out, face in the direction of travel, pick
flat terrain and jump with your knees bent, ready to hit the ground

running in the direction of the train." The train-jumping training worked and we arrived at the crew shed in one piece.

The crew barracks had two dormitories. The larger room housed a half-dozen Polish workers from our firm. The smaller housed our "security force" of four Germans: Fritz, a redheaded sergeant with some experience in construction who was the overall boss man, and three privates who did sentry duty. I mostly did plain unskilled labor since there was not all that much translating to do. Fritz and the Polish foreman communicated well enough with grunts and curses. Soon Fritz gave me an additional assignment. I became a part-time "gofer" between the construction site and the Kiev office. Fortunately, I did not have to learn how to jump onto a moving train. Fritz had a red signal flag and the authority to stop trains. When needed, I would pick up mail, payroll, reports, and complaints. Unofficially, I would also buy stuff for the crew, mostly on the black market, since you could buy nothing at the construction site.

I became an expert train jumper and cargo handler. I also learned a lot about opportunities and hazards of train travel. The cars for local civilians, if present at all, were constantly harassed by Ukrainian Police security patrols that checked identity papers and belongings for black market items. The Reich Germans' compartments were checked by military police for papers but not for contraband. While working on the tower I wore old civilian clothes, but when traveling on the railroad, I wore my Organization Todt uniform. My firm's Travel Orders combined with the uniform worked just fine in the Reich Germans' Only compartment.

I stayed at Marek's place while in Kiev. The newlyweds seemed to get along well. I asked Marek if Katia knew anything about his background. "No way," said Marek. "How about your circumcision?" "She's not that good at comparative anatomy," he assured me. He described how he completed his second transport from Lvov and smuggled in four Jews. His main problem, he explained, was how to keep the Poles in the transport from recognizing the Jews. His next transport was going to be Jews only. "You are just worrying about the Poles," I volunteered, "but Germans are no fools." "The

Germans cannot tell a Pole from a Jew as well as the Poles can," said Marek. I told him that the plan was risky. "You're right," he agreed. "I will pull this one off and I will get out of the transport business."

In April, the weather became nicer at the construction site and the ever-present mud began to dry out. At the crack of dawn one Sunday on our day off, a few of the Polish workers, including me, hired a horse-drawn cart from a local farmer for a trip to Vinnitsa. I was surprised to see quite a bit of German military traffic in town. Unknown to me at the time, Hitler had one of his underground field headquarters built near Vinnitsa. I might have been just a few miles from him!

We went to an open-air bazaar. This was not only a place to buy things, but also a good spot for socializing and getting news. The variety of food and the relatively low prices, as compared to Kiev, were quite noticeable. The talkative tradesmen explained that most of the goods were smuggled from Transnistria, the region of the Ukraine between the rivers Dnestr and Bug that included the Black Sea port of Odessa. The Germans gave this area to Romania for its participation in the war. The Romanian occupation was much more lax than the German occupation. There was a lot more food available for the population. Here at the bazaar, I found out for the first time that the Romanian and Italian armies had been destroyed in the prelude to Stalingrad. Now I understood the significance of the Italian deserters in the Kiev bazaar, the previous December, who were trading their guns for food.

We did our shopping, had a good meal and a few drinks of vodka, and headed back in the afternoon. About fifteen miles out of Vinnitsa, while we were traveling through the woods, a squad of Soviet partisans armed with submachine guns ambushed us. They surrounded the cart and demanded that we raise our hands. We quickly obliged. "Hey, comrades," we assured them. "Don't shoot. We are Poles. We are on your side!" The partisans tied our hands behind our backs and pulled the cart off the road. They wanted to know what a bunch of Poles were doing in the middle of the war, in the middle of a Ukrainian forest. I said in Russian: "we are building a railroad water tower so that when we are finished, you can blow it up again." The partisan commandant didn't think that my remark was particularly funny, but he was interested and he interrogated us in detail about the German security detachment and progress at the site. We obliged him with even the smallest of details: the routines of sentries, the location of the weapons and ammunition, and the construction schedule.

During the interrogation, I had the feeling that the commandant knew a lot about us and seemed to even know the pet name of the horse. It looked to me like the farmer from whom we had hired the cart reported our planned trip. The partisans searched our wagon and took all of our bazaar purchases. They were particularly delighted with ten gallons of samogon, a home made, foul-tasting and potent potato-distilled vodka. The commandant assured us: "If you say one word about this encounter to the Germans, we will kill you the next time we pay a visit to your water tower." He untied our hands and gave us back the horse-drawn cart, and let us go. The fact that they let us keep the cart confirmed my conviction that the cart's owner was working with the partisans. Our only problem was that the money for half of the samogon vodka came from the German crew. As the interpreter, I had to explain it to Fritz. I told him that the money was stolen from us at the bazaar. "Liar, liar," he yelled. "What did you do with vodka?" He slapped my face hard. I stuck to my story. Finally, Fritz pronounced that he would take the German crew's money out of our pay. I agreed; a cheap price to pay compared to getting shot by the partisans. I was convinced that now, since the partisans found out about the rather pitiful German defenses of the tower, they would pay us a visit soon. It would be goodbye tower and goodbye Fritz, goodbye and good riddance.

On my next trip to Kiev, I stopped first at Katia and Marek's apartment. The apartment was a mess; Katia was in a panic, her eyes red from crying. She pushed me quickly through the front room, out of view from the street, and into the kitchen. She was hysterical and quite visibly pregnant. It took awhile for her to calm down and tell me the gruesome story. There was some problem with the transport at the Lvov railroad station. The Gestapo grabbed Marek and his whole group from the train. The Kiev Gestapo was notified and they had raided the Kurt Wuttge office two days ago. Everybody was interrogated, including the German manager. Most were released except for three that the Gestapo said were Jews and two others. Romek was one of them. These five were shot.

The Gestapo paid Katia a visit the previous day and ransacked the apartment. "They asked me about you," warned Katia. "Don't go to the office." That made good sense. The Gestapo had a way of extracting information from even the most reluctant prisoners. It was very likely that Marek was tortured and told them all he knew before they killed him. I told Katia that she, too, must leave Kiev and that I would help her. I did not think that Katia realized, even now, that Marek was Jewish and so she could be accused of harboring a Jew. She said, "I cannot leave now. How can I have a child on the run without my family?" In any case, she reasoned, "If they had wanted to arrest me, they would have done it yesterday." This made some sense since she was very pregnant and still free, so I did not press the escape any further. Neither did I tell her that Marek was Jewish. If he did not want her to know, it was not my place to tell. In case it mattered, she could truthfully say that she did not know that Marek was a Jew. I thanked her for the warning, hugged her good bye, and we parted. I found out later that Katia was arrested the next day and no one ever saw her again.

Chapter 10

Dash to Odessa

The news of Marek's arrest was a powerful shock. He was my only friend in this new life and my one contact with the past. Without Marek, Edwin Langberg did not exist. Only Leslaw Strutinski survived and Leslaw's future was now in question. The consequences of Marek's arrest were disastrous for everyone involved with him. Was Marek a fallen hero or an adventurer who cost many people their lives? I settled for a hero since he was at least trying to do something constructive, even if he was doing well by doing good. Besides, there was no time to dwell on his fate. I was in trouble, deep trouble and I had to think very carefully about my next move.

First, I needed a safe place to think. I headed for the *bania*, Kiev's municipal bathhouse. Unlike contemporary bathhouses in the western world, the bania in Kiev served its intended function. In the Ukraine, a bathroom in the home was a rarity, so most people took a fortnightly steam bath and shower at the bania -- whether they needed it or not. I paid the entrance fee to the bania and received a locker key. The attendant looked at my green Organization Todt uniform and my travel bag, too small for a change of laundry, with some curiosity. The changing room was big and partitioned with wooden benches and lockers. Dozens of men in different stages of dress and undress didn't nearly fill the room. I found a place near a window and took off my conspicuous uniform. Partially dressed I felt better disguised. Now, no one paid the slightest attention to me. Good place.

What should I do? The Gestapo was clearly looking for me. By now, Fritz would have received a message from them to detain me at the construction site. He would have informed them that I was headed for Kiev on business. They would be looking for me at the Kurt Wuttge office in Kiev, right now. When I did not show up, they would widen the search. I could fill out one of my blank Travel Orders and hop on a train. But then, I remembered from my travels that when the German Military Police checked ID papers, they glanced down at a list. I never thought about it before, but now I realized that it must contain the names of wanted people. The name of Leslaw Strutinski would now be on it.

I figured that the list was likely to be alphabetical. A change from **S**trutinski to **H**rutinski on my ID pass would change the position on the list. I discretely emptied my travel bag and tore open the false bottom, to get to the First Aid Kit. I looked around; no one was looking at me. I took out the liquid ink eraser and carefully read the instructions. I put a drop on the S and let it do its magic for a few minutes, until the ink dissolved and the paper didn't. I carefully blotted the paper and then, let it dry. The S did not disappear completely but it would have to be examined very carefully in order to see the remains. I took out the pen and the vial of document ink from the kit. I drew an H where the S used to be, steadying my hand as best I could and blotted the excess ink. I put my belongings into the locker to give the doctored ID pass a chance to dry. I hoped and prayed that the forgery would look better dry than it did at this moment of creation.

I took a long steam bath and shower while trying to figure out my new escape destination. Transnistria seemed like my best bet, since Romanians administered it and a change in jurisdiction would improve my chances of survival. Besides, I had heard some good things about life in Transnistria when I was at the bazaar in Vinnitsa. Back in the dressing room, I looked again at my doctored ID paper.

The ink had dried the same color as the rest. The paper was a little discolored around the H but it was likely to pass a routine check. I then took out a blank Travel Order and sent Leslaw **Hrutinski** to his new destination: a railroad construction project in Odessa.

From the bania I went to the Kiev bazaar, the black-market haven that I knew well, and bought a military-looking rubberized raincoat made in Germany. The raincoat was expensive but it was worth every ruble because when I put it on, it covered my green Organization Todt uniform, a likely item in my fugitive description. I headed for the Kiev railroad station and bought a copy of *Das Schwarze Korps* (The Black Order), the official newspaper of the SS. I stuck the paper into the pocket of my newly acquired coat, making sure that the skull and cross bones on the paper banner were visible.

The station was bustling with German troops. I had to wait for a tense hour and then I got into the Reich-Germans-Only compartment on the next train to Odessa. I knew this railway line well, because it went past the construction site. Fortunately, I didn't see anyone that I knew. As expected, about a half-hour out of Kiev, the MPs with their distinctive gladiator-like metal breast plates came in for the Travel Order check. I took a deep breath and let it out very slowly.

I nonchalantly handed my Travel Order and ID pass to the MP. He looked at the Travel Order and then at his list, and then he looked again at the Travel Order. He did not hand it back to me. He consulted his partner. I was terrified but tried not to show it. "Your Travel Order is incorrect," he informed me. "You need a special permit to travel outside the *Reichskommissari*at to Transnistria." I obligingly said that I would go back to my firm and tell them to get the necessary permit. "No," said the MP emphatically. "You will proceed directly and without delay, as ordered. *We* will notify your firm and tell them what to do." He wrote down my name and the firm's name and address and moved on. I was relieved that they let me go but I knew that in a few days, the Gestapo would know that I was in Odessa under the name of Hrutinski.

The train passed the construction site, stopped in Vinnitsa, and soon after reached the last station under German administration. My compartment emptied out. The MPs checked the papers of the remaining few passengers in the Luftwaffe and Kriegsmarine uniforms heading for the German airfield and port facilities in Odessa. The MPs recognized me from earlier and just passed me by. They got off the train and took off the Reich-Germans-Only sign and waited on the platform until the train left. In another hour, we reached the first station in Romanian-occupied Transnistria. The change was dramatic. The train filled up with new passengers, mostly local civilians. In amazement, I watched food vendors peddling meat-filled piroshki to the passengers. Finally, I could take off the German raincoat and pitch the SS newspaper. The conductor told me to go out and get a ticket at the counter, maybe just to prove that German Travel Orders did not impress him. There was no more oppressive and deadly German efficiency; instead there was a cozy feeling that no one gave a damn. I arrived in Odessa late at night and, like other travelers waiting out the night curfew, I slept till morning in the station.

In the morning, I wandered about the city. A circular plaza in front of the railroad station led to a wide boulevard. Odessa is a Crimean port city on the Black Sea. The Germans and Romanians had surrounded the city in 1941 and, after two months of bitter resistance by the outnumbered Soviet troops, conquered it. Predictably, the large pre-war Jewish population of Odessa that numbered 180,000 vanished by the time I was there. Some were drafted into the Red Army, some escaped with the Soviets, but most were killed or deported by the Nazis. Now, men in German uniforms, mostly Luftwaffe, were few and far between, and doing their best to maintain their swagger. The uniformed Romanians looked like they would rather make love than participate in a losing war. Romanians were a strange lot.

As an ally of Germany, Romania declared war on the USSR in 1941. The Romanian Army advanced into southern Ukraine occupying the region beyond the former border on the river Dnestr up to the river Bug, a region that included Odessa. The Romanian Army had its own version of the German Einsatzgruppe killing squads, called the Special Echalon. They massacred more than 40,000 Jewish civilians in Odessa on October 27, 1941. In the late fall of 1942, the Third Romanian Army took the brunt of the Soviet attack, attempting to defend the northern flank of the Stalingrad front. Within days, the Romanian Army collapsed under this attack. This, in turn, led to the encirclement of the German Fifth Army in the Battle of Stalingrad, a pivotal German defeat. The Romanian rout was a source of bitter recrimination and seriously weakened the alliance.

Another source of contention was the German attitude of racial and cultural superiority. Ethnically, the Romanians were a mixed breed and there was some indication that the Gypsies and many Romanians were related. In any case, Romania had a large Gypsy minority. Gypsies, like Jews were on Hitler's extermination list. Germans contemptuously referred to Romanians as *Ciganervolke* (a nation of gypsies). Romanians treated their own internal Jewish minority with spontaneous old-fashioned pogroms. Comically, this offended Nazi sensibility. The Nazis disparaged pogroms as a barbaric and undisciplined display. Still, a much higher percentage of Romanian Jews survived the war as compared with the German Jews who were treated to Nazi 'civilization'.

Back to the spring of 1943: In spite of the war devastation, I was struck by the beauty of Odessa and could understand why it was called the "Pearl of the Black Sea." The spring weather and warm climate brought lush green vegetation to the ruins of bombed-out houses that remained standing after the conquest. The vegetation was a strange reminder that life goes on. I could see that many of the ruins must have once been impressive architectural masterpieces, as were their gardens and parks. The Potemkin Steps were part of a most unusual terraced street. In spite of its proximity to the Ukraine, the local language spoken in Odessa was Russian.

Love in Odessa

By mid-morning, I got hungry and stopped at a small restaurant to have something to eat. One could not only get food but also local wine, and of course, the ever-present, smelly samogon vodka. The restaurant had black market prices, but it was not all that black since it had a sign and was run quite openly. As I ate, I racked my brain for a workable plan. I had succeeded in getting out of the region of direct German occupation, yet I realized that most of my acquired survival skills were geared to knowing the Germans, their language and the way they operated. I wondered how I could use this knowledge to survive in Odessa. I remembered the Luftwaffe officers on the train and their talk about a German-run airfield. I decided to explore this possibility. I would go to the German airfield to find out if they needed a pair of hands with some drafting and construction experience. My cover story would be that I was sent to a railroad construction site, but due to unforeseen delays, work had not begun. In the meantime, I needed some gainful employment. In view of the ever-present labor shortages, especially of German-speaking labor, they just might be interested at the airfield. I would not fill out any applications then and there because I could not use the name Hrutinski any more. If the prospects look good, I would use my newly acquired forging skills to concoct a new identity.

There was a fair amount of truck traffic on the road to the airfield and I hitched a ride. The airfield was a sprawling installation, some ten miles outside of Odessa, in the midst of ripening cantaloupe fields. I was directed to the Employment Office. "Yes" was the answer, they could certainly use me, but they required clearance from the German Komendantur in Odessa. The Employment Office even arranged a ride for me in a truck that was going there. I decided to play along. Not that I was going to show them my Hrutinski papers, but just to find out if the clearance was likely to be an easy routine or a thorough check.

I was asking a burly corporal in the Security Section what I needed for the clearance when he abruptly ushered me to see his superior officer, Leutnant Schmidt. I had no chance to protest this unforeseen development. (Leutnant Schmidt is imbedded in my memory of things German. I can't bring myself now to translate his rank to Lieutenant. In a perfectly-fitting SS uniform, he was a picture of a Nazi "superman"). Leutnant Schmidt eyed me up and down. Standing at attention, I told him my cover story. "Let me see your papers," he demanded. "As I was explaining to the corporal, I don't have them with me, but I will bring them to you." "What do you mean walking without ID papers? Where do you think you are?" He was ready to pounce, but he then leaned back. Maybe he answered his own question. We were in Odessa and the Romanians were supposed to be in charge. "Come right back here with your papers," he yelled and dismissed me. I knew that I had no chance of passing his scrutiny with my amateur forgeries and thin cover stories. I was really lucky that Leutnant Schmidt did not detain me, right there and then. I was glad to be out on the street and out of his reach. Little did I know that the scary Leutnant and I would meet again soon, very soon.

Chapter 11

Counter-Espionage Prison

The airfield "inquiry" was sloppy and I could have kicked myself for taking such a chance. Back in the city, I had my evening meal at a bigger restaurant. This one provided more than just food and booze; there were women drinking alone at the bar. I concocted a new, somewhat short-term plan. I made eye contact with one of the women and we struck up a conversation. "Yes," she said. She was interested, for a price, provided I had a room. Clearly, this was not what I had in mind. The second contact was much better. "Why don't you get a bottle of vodka and some food and we will go to my place." The bottle of vodka was three times as much as the price of the first lady, but this plan was worth it.

Natasha took me to her apartment. It consisted of one room and a tiny kitchen that she shared with her mother. Natasha was in her late twenties, her looks fading fast. We talked. Her mother was out in the countryside visiting her sister for a couple of weeks. Natasha was now a full-time alcoholic and a part-time prostitute to support her addiction. She had not seen her husband since he was drafted into the Soviet Army two years earlier. Their 5-year old daughter had died of pneumonia the previous winter. After her death, Natasha started drinking heavily and hated to be alone.

I told her my "construction in Odessa" cover story. I was sure that she did not believe it, but she did not ask me any questions since she was delighted that I was just looking for a place to stay and not for sex. We made a deal: I would provide the food and the booze. She would cook for me and I could sleep in her mother's bed. We had a real win - win situation. If all went well, my First Aid Kit emergency funds would keep the deal going for a few weeks. Everything should be fine until either I ran out of money or Natasha's mother returned and claimed her bed.

The next day, I visited a bazaar and acquired locally made civilian clothes, shoes, and underwear. In Odessa, my Organization Todt uniform was a distinctive, eye-catching liability. I stored my uniform and newly acquired belongings at Natasha's place. She watched my transformation and asked me nothing. Our silent understanding worked. In Odessa, the population spoke Russian or Ukrainian. I asked how they handled official applications to the Romanian authorities since no one knew Romanian. She told me about translator businesses that specialized in such things.

I needed a new, local identity. Could I somehow or other, with the help of a "cooperative" translator, figure out a way to get appropriate ID papers and stay in Odessa? The trick was to find someone that I could trust to be crooked. By now, I realized that my cover story was not worth much. I had to find someone who was willing to ask no questions and come up with the right answers. I still had my father's gold watch in the First Aid Kit to use as a sweetener. It was time to window shop for the right translator.

Natasha gave me directions to a nearby translation office. The man in the office was a middle-aged Romanian who spoke good Russian. To get a feel for the situation, I tried out my window-shopping story that I wanted to visit my family in another town, and how much would such an application for a travel permit cost? He gave me an estimate. My vibes about the man were neutral. I decided to move on until I felt distinctly positive vibes. For several days, I continued to look for a "creative" translator. Not being a mind reader, it was hard to determine who would be the right person who would not simply pocket my watch and do nothing for me... or worse.

I had another exotic idea. Since Odessa was a port on the northern coast of the Black Sea and Turkey was a neutral country on the south coast of the Black Sea, maybe there would be traffic between the two. Could I stow away on a ship? Maybe a fishing boat would take me on? The next day I checked it out, but my trip to the port of Odessa was very disappointing. An imposing guarded gate closed the road to the port facilities and the facility was fenced off by high barbed wire with big signs suggesting that trespassing was punishable by death. In my civilian clothing, even if I had the inclination, there was no way for me to enter the German-operated port facility. In any case, there were no signs of any commercial shipping, no ships going to Turkey, and no fishing boats, just the German Navy. I was dejected and beginning to doubt the whole Odessa move.

In the late afternoon while walking back to Natasha's place, I saw another translator's office. "I might as well give it another try," I thought. The office had a neatly decorated storefront. The only person in there was a young, shapely blond. I asked her for a quotation for the permit job and she said the Romanian woman who ran the shop was gone for the day. "You will have to come tomorrow," she said. "Are you about to close," I gulped. "Yes," she said, "in about fifteen minutes." Her name was Tatiana. "Do you mind if I walk you home?" Tatiana agreed. I was very delighted and my delight had nothing to do with my translator search. I could not take my eyes off Tatiana. It was the first time since my Kiev escape that I was preoccupied with a thought other than survival.

Tatiana and I walked, talked, and enjoyed each other's company. I suggested that we have dinner together that evening. She readily accepted. We had a carefree meal and a bottle of wine in a local restaurant. We acted as if there was no war. Tatiana was a high school student before the 1941 German invasion, but now, two years later at 17, she and her mother had to work to support the family. Her father was somewhere in the Soviet Army. After dinner, we stopped in a park and kissed, and hugged, and let our senses take over.

Tatiana wanted to know about me. I did not dare to tell her the whole truth but I did not want to lie either. I told her that I had escaped from Lvov to Kiev and from Kiev to Odessa, hinting that the reason was political. She sensed my reluctance to provide details and did not press the subject. "Maybe my boss can help you; I will talk to her without mentioning your name," she volunteered. "Can you trust her," I asked breathlessly. "She would not hurt me," Tatiana assured me. We made another date for the next evening.

Early the next day, Tatiana talked to her Romanian boss. She was willing to help, but she wanted to meet me the next day. I brought her my father's gold watch. The boss, an energetic Romanian woman in her forties, said she knew a police official who had done similar "favors" for her. In exchange for the gold watch, I would get ID papers to allow me to stay in Odessa. "No questions asked," I wondered aloud. "No questions asked?" she assured me. I had a long, last look at the gold watch. I gave it to the Romanian woman and hoped that my father would understand. She gave me directions to the police headquarters and wrote the name of the police official that I was to meet. "See him at 9 a.m. tomorrow," she instructed. I met with Tatiana again that evening. We were very happy that I would be able to stay in Odessa and continue our relationship.

The next morning at the appointed time, I walked to the police headquarters, in great spirits. I went into the office of the bribed official to pick up my papers. He said he was expecting me, and he asked how I got to Odessa. Since I thought that I had him in my pocket, I told him, without hesitation, about my train trip from Kiev. A dark look came over his face: "Can I see your papers?" he asked. I wondered why a bribed man would ask me so many questions. "Maybe he just had to keep up appearances," I consoled myself. I reluctantly handed over my Hrutinski ID paper and Travel Order. The official slowly wrote down my statement. I really began to worry when he asked me to sign it. Then, he called "Guard!"

The guard brusquely handcuffed me and pushed me from behind, out of the office. He escorted me from police headquarters to a stark, fenced-in building several blocks away and delivered me to the prison office. I was processed and a guard brought me to a cell. The lock clunked behind me. I was now an inmate in the Romanian counter-espionage prison in Odessa.

A small window, secured with heavy iron bars dimly lit the 30 by 40-foot cell. Across from the entrance, two-tiered wooden bunks, covered with straw, were mounted the full length of the wall. Wooden benches and a table completed the furniture. There were five other prisoners in the cell, in their twenties and thirties. Two of my cellmates played chess with pieces made from bread, on a penciled board. They stopped and looked at me with curiosity. A man who seemed to be the oldest of the five inmates greeted me: "My name is Grisha," he said. "I am the host here, responsible for introductions." Grisha was a short man with dark, slightly graying hair and a commanding presence. With a bow and a wave of the hand, he parodied an actor on a stage. I could not help but smile. These guys were no ordinary pickpockets, I thought. And indeed they were not. They didn't talk much about what got them there, but it was a safe bet however that they were Soviet operatives caught by the Romanians in Transnistria. My cellmates questioned me a bit, but not to find out who I really was - that was taboo in the cell - but to make sure that the Romanians did not plant me. Based on my accent, it was clear that I was from Poland. Adding the fact that I was only 18 and lacked experience in prison matters, in about a day, they decided that I was OK.

Life in the cell was monotony, interrupted by terror. One of the prisoners was led away and did not return. Another was taken away and returned in a few hours beaten and bruised. Grisha explained to me that we were in a holding cell. Some prisoners were kept here for a few weeks and some for a few days, while interrogators were working on each case and deciding on a treatment. It was clear that the treatment could be harsh. We could hear muffled screams. Grisha tried to keep up our morale. He taught Russian literature before the war in an Odessa high school and was trying to distract us by quoting poetry and telling stories. When I climbed on a bench to see through the window into the prison yard, I saw scaffolding for hanging. I could also see swallows circling in the sky, unperturbed by the barbed wire fences and bars. Oh, if I could only fly!

Some of the prisoners got food parcels from friends or relatives, smuggled in by bribing the guards. Grisha wanted to know if I had any family in Odessa. I told him that I did not. "Then I hope you like *mamalyga*," he commented. Mamalyga was a bland corn mush. We were served watery soup for lunch and mamalyga for breakfast and dinner. On the third day of incarceration, I got a food package sent by Tatiana. This strengthened my feeling that it was not Tatiana who betrayed me. I shared the package with my cellmates and could sense that their respect for me moved from low to one notch higher.

On day four, I had my first interrogation. The interrogating officer was a Romanian Army Captain in his thirties. The room was sparse: a desk, a few chairs, and a filing cabinet. The interrogation was in Russian, which he spoke fluently. He had my Hrutinski ID pass, my Travel Order, and my signed confession in front of him. I repeated the same story, giving "a better life" as the reason for my trip to Odessa. "You should be able to make up a better story than that, Hrudinsky," he said. He wanted to know who sent me to Odessa and why. I told him, as it happened truthfully, that I just came there of my own volition. After an hour, the interrogation ended. I was sent back to the holding cell and I told Grisha about the experience.

On day seven, I was brought before my interrogator again. The captain seemed more cordial this time. He told me that he had met with Tatiana and her boss and he was inclined to believe that my stay in Odessa was more a question of love than war. Under the circumstances, the Romanian authorities were going to release me. However, since I came from Lvov and Kiev, I was not really under their jurisdiction and so they were going to release me to the German authorities. "What German authorities?" I wanted to know. "The German Commandantour in Odessa," he answered. "By the way," the captain added, pointing to the H in Hrutinski, "you should have done a better job. You will be glad to know that I said nothing about this in my report." That was very small consolation. I remembered Leutnant Schmidt. I was sure that by now Marek's case and the Strutinski-Hrutinski story were in the Odessa Gestapo files. And even if they were not there, Leutnant Schmidt was surely going to inquire about my background.

When I returned to the cell, I again told Grisha about the interrogation. I told him that I would much rather try an escape, no matter how risky, than be delivered to the Gestapo. Grisha consulted with another cellmate, a native of Odessa. "We will try to help you but you must first swear that you will never squeal." "Never," I assured him. "On your mother's life..." "My mother is dead," I muttered. "Is your father alive?" "Yes, I hope so; he is somewhere with the Soviets," I said. "Then swear on your father's life." I swore.

The three of us worked on a plan. They told me where, on the way to the German Commandantour, I would be passing a block of bombed-out buildings. This was my best chance to escape. They explained where to run to evade the guard, and gave me the address and directions to a safe house where I could hide, provided I was not being followed, and a code word to use when I got there. "We are helping you now," said Grisha. "In the unlikely event that you survive, we will expect you to do some things for us." "It's a deal," I agreed. "Who is *us*?" I asked. "We are fighting for the King of Greece," said Grisha with his usual sarcastic sense of humor, figuring that I knew perfectly well that he was a Soviet agent.

In the late afternoon, I was taken to a guardhouse. A skinny Romanian soldier in an ill-fitting private's uniform, armed with a rifle with a bayonet attached, was assigned as my escort. I knew from Grisha that we had about a half-hour's walk. The guard spoke some broken Russian. I tried to pretend to be delighted that I was finally being released to my friends the Germans. We reached the bombed-out block of buildings and I asked the guard for permission to relieve myself. He pointed to a corner and waved me on. I reached the corner and started running as fast as I could. He could not have been more than 30 feet away and yelled "Stop!" I kept running. I heard the click of his gun but no shot. He either hadn't loaded the gun or the cartridge was defective. This trick of fate saved my life because at this distance, he could not have missed.

With the guard in hot pursuit, I kept running towards a major busy street. The guard had a police whistle and started blowing it. This started a commotion with Russians yelling encouragements and an old woman who started wailing. I guess I reminded her of the death of her sons. Suddenly, a young boy, maybe twelve in a Hitler youth uniform, stuck out his foot and tripped me. I fell and hit the pavement hard and slid for a few feet before coming to a stop. My hands and knees were bloody. The impact on my belly, combined with diarrhea caused by the jail diet, made my bowels explode.

In seconds, the guard caught up with me and started beating me with the butt of his rifle. He cuffed my hands behind my back, and with a piece of rope, tied the handcuffs to his belt. The rope was short enough so that his bayonet touched my back. It was obviously quite a sight because pedestrians stopped and gawked. I was completely dejected; I had expected to either be shot by the guard or maybe with luck, to have escaped. But now, the worst had happened. I was being led, alive, to the Gestapo and I had no illusions that my death there would be much more painful.

We reached the security office of the Commandantour at about 6 p.m., close to quitting time. The Romanian guard handed my transfer papers to the same burly corporal that I met before. The corporal looked at the papers and then at my state and asked the guard for an explanation. The Romanian knew no German so standing two fingers against the desk top he tried to produce the figure of a man running. He kept saying: *fuga, fuga.* I was just standing there dazed when I realized that maybe I could act as an "interpreter" between the two.

I spoke up: "I was trying to run to the toilet when the Romanian caught me and beat me up." Leutnant Schmidt walked out of his office looking like he was ready for a beer after a busy day. When he saw me, he stopped; obviously annoyed that shit was dripping down my pant leg onto his spotlessly clean office floor. He wanted to know from the corporal what on earth was going on. "The Romanians released the prisoner because he is in our jurisdiction. He got beaten up by the guard on the way." Herr Leutnant gave me a sharp look. "Have I seen you before?" he asked me in German. In spite of my aching body, I stood at attention and decided to improve on the truth: "Yes, Herr Leutnant, a few weeks ago, I was here to get my stay in Odessa approved by you, but before I had a chance to get my papers back to you, the Romanians arrested me." Herr Leutnant nodded to the corporal, "Yes, I talked to him." Then Herr Leutnant left the office, probably because my smell was ruining his appetite for dinner. That left the corporal to handle the smelly situation. He figured that if Herr Leutnant talked to me about my stay in Odessa, it must be OK. He stamped a pass with a permission to stay in Odessa and handed me the papers.

The Romanian guard looked at this development in dismay, shook his head, and started yelling in Romanian repeating, *fuga, fuga*. The corporal pointed at the door and told him to leave, but the Romanian refused. Not to be outdone, the corporal cursed him: "*Verdammte Ciganervolke!*" The Romanian persisted. The burly corporal got annoyed and kicked the skinny Romanian out of the office. Then he offered me parting advice: "You, too, get out on the double and, man, take a good bath." I was free, back on the streets of Odessa.

I limped the three blocks that separated me from the sea. There was no beach but a bombed-out waterfront warehouse would do nicely. I stripped and washed my clothes in the seawater. While my clothes were drying in the sun, I floated in the sea. The cool water felt good against my aches and pains. My awful smell was gone. I let the incredible course of events sink in. I was alive, and except for painful bruises and cuts, I did not appear to be seriously damaged. As I floated, I closed my eyes and tried to bring to mind the image of my grandmother to thank her for interceding for me in yet another rescue. The process of bringing up her image in my mind was not easy. I had to get beyond my Leslaw identity and think again about

93

Edwin whom I really needed to forget. In my mind, I had to move past the Ghetto gates and past the memories of the Nazis, the black-shirt Ukrainians and the Judenrat. I remembered the annihilation of Jews that was ignominiously passive and unnecessarily easy for the Nazis. I finally reached the image of Sara, sitting in her bed, propped up by the pillows and radiating courage: "You will survive the war, Grandson." I gave my thanks for her blessing.

I knew then that if I wanted to live with myself for the rest of my life without guilt and shame, I must make myself worthy of having been saved. I realized there are times when thinking only about self-preservation is a coward's way out. Now would be one of those times. There would be no more hiding in Odessa to wait out the war. I survived and I would keep my promise to Grisha, even though I was free and I did not need him now. I would keep my promise even though I despised the communist police-state life style. Through Grisha's contact, I finally had the chance to join the fight and I would. I felt that this was the only way that I could be worthy.

When my clothes were reasonably dry, I got dressed. But before I met with Grisha's contact, I had a painful walk back to my previous "landlord" Natasha's place. She was home and so was her mother. Natasha did not ask too many questions, but her mother was not kindly disposed towards me. "Oh, you are the new customer that she is whoring with." I explained that sometimes appearances are misleading and Natasha confirmed the platonic nature of our deal. The daughter's virtue pleased her mother. So she thought of me as the fool who pays for the goods, and instead of enjoying them, leaves and gets beaten up. In any case, considering my state, they agreed to let me stay in their kitchen. As long as the mother kept her bed, there was peace. The next day, I made contact with Grisha's safe house and moved out.

Chapter 12

Working for the Underground

My contact was a waiter in a greasy-spoon restaurant in a working-class district of Odessa. The code words were simple: "Grisha sent me."

The waiter gave me some food and vodka. Vania, my handler, came in about a half-hour. He told me that when I did not show up as expected the day before, they gave me up for lost. He asked me to tell my real story, "no bullshit, please." I told him the truth: I was Edwin Langberg, an escaped Jew from Drohobycz. I told him about Marek's capture and my flight from Kiev, about Tatiana and the bribe that misfired. He enjoyed the story of my narrow escape from the Commandantour. "The corporal is sure going to lose his cushy job in Odessa and end up on the Eastern front when they find out that he released an escaped Jew, wanted in Kiev," Vania laughed. *Molodets* (good young man, in loose translation); he had given me a backhanded complement in Russian.

I told Vania that I promised Grisha to pay off my debt for his help. "Are you sure?" he looked at me sharply. I nodded. "You must understand that the less you know about us, the better. There is always a risk that you may be caught. You ask no unnecessary questions and do as you are told. You will be gone for a good while.

Is there anyone in Odessa that you want to say goodbye to?" he wanted to know. "I would like to see Tatiana before I leave." "This is out of the question. It is only a matter of time until they find out that they should not have released you. The first place they will be watching is Tatiana's. Write her and after you are safely out of here, we will give her your letter." This made sense and I agreed.

Vania had a horse-drawn cart with some boxes covered by straw. He gave me a lift to Natasha's, where I picked up my belongings -- including Sara's diary -- and I said my quick good-byes to Natasha and her mother. Vania was quite interested in my blank Travel Orders and made sure that I had them with me. He blindfolded me and said apologetically, "remember, the less you know the safer it is." I lay in the wagon, covered with straw. I bounced around for about an hour before we got to our destination. It was a carpentry shop, somewhere on the outskirts of Odessa. My new quarters were a room in the attic with a bunk bed, a large table, and a few chairs. Two of the boxes from the cart were brought up and unpacked on the table. One box had a two-way field radio; the other was filled with spare parts and manuals. The radio was of German manufacture and the manuals were in German. "We blew up a Romanian supply train and "liberated" a shipment of ten German radios and a lot of other good things. You tell me you know German and you know something about electricity. See if you can figure out how to operate these radios and teach our men to use them," Vania commanded.

I read the manuals but there were a lot of technical terms I did not understand. The radio could be operated by cranking bicycle-like pedals or by connecting it to a vehicle battery. I told Vania I needed a battery or a helper to crank the pedals. To my delight, the help was a radio operator trained in Morse code. I don't know how Vania got him and I knew better than to ask too many questions. He knew more about radios than I did, but I knew German so we were a good team. Thankfully the parts box had a dummy antenna so that we could test the transmitter without sending out any unwanted signals. We had the first radio going and tested within two days. The radio operator took it a few miles away from our building and successfully transmitted an operational message. Vania was very pleased and we celebrated over a bottle of vodka.

Over the next few days, we had eight out of the ten radios working. We trained and equipped one more radio operator. The last two radios probably needed a tube replacement but even though we had spare tubes, we did not have a tube tester. As we were working on the last two radios, Vania told us to hurry up the testing, and one way or another, finish it by the end of the day.

The next day, the operator and I left for Berezovka, a town some 50 miles north of Odessa with all the operational radios except for one, left behind for local use. Our mission was to distribute the radios and train more operators in the use of the German equipment. Vania told me that he found out through the grapevine, that the Romanians were actively looking for me. I was to take all my belongings with me because I would not be returning to Odessa. He obtained local ID papers that justified this one journey for the radio operator and me.

The following morning, Vania wished us luck and we took off in a horse-drawn cart. No blindfolds this time. The radio operator knew the back roads and got us to our destination, a farm near Berezovka, without any problems. Four radio operators attended our "class" and left with their equipment. I was told the next distribution point was Nicolaev and I was to go there by myself. Nikolaev is about 60 miles southeast of Berezovka on the eastern side of the river Bug, the border of Transnistria. This was bad news. I would be outside the Romanian administration and under the Germans again.

Since civilian traffic was severely restricted on the river Bug Bridge, I would have to smuggle the radios across it. I was told to get back into my Organization Todt uniform and to write myself another of my Leslaw Hrutinski Travel Orders (what else). The partisan commandant of Berezovka told me that Vania had high hopes for this plan: "It worked for you before," he was trying to convince me. "No reason why it should not work again." "But they are looking for me now," I objected. "Ah, you are not that important," the commandant snapped. "They may be looking for you in Odessa, but they're not going to be looking for you on the train to Nikolayev. Anyway, you volunteered and these are your orders. Work out the details."

How could I possibly conceal two German radios? The only place I could think of was... under their noses. I decided to blatantly keep the radios in their original boxes and to write on my Travel Order the true purpose of my trip: to deliver the boxes, even though the delivery was to quite a different customer.

It was now early in September, 1943. The tide of German victories had turned. On the Eastern front, after the debacle at Stalingrad early that year, the Germans tried to recover their initiative in the July battle of Kursk. There the Germans lost the biggest tank battle of World War II.

From where I was in September, the front was still 400 miles east, at the very northeast tip of the Sea of Azov. But a big push against the Germans was brewing. The German and Romanian troops occupying the Taman peninsula and the Crimea were in danger of being cut off as the Soviet offensive moved along the northern coast of the Sea of Azov towards Nicolaev. The objective of the partisans was to harass German transportation from the rear.

The attitude of the local population had undergone a dramatic change. The initial Ukrainian euphoria about the German "liberation" from the communist and Russian domination melted away as the reality sunk in that Hitler's plan was not to free but to colonize the Ukraine. From the occupied territories, about three million young civilians of both sexes were deported to work as slave labor in German industry. In general, they were treated badly, undernourished, and were driven and bullied until many of them dropped dead. These deportations encouraged local people to flee from their homes and to join the partisans. Soviet soldiers who were cut off during the early retreats and managed to survive in the woods, supplemented the partisan contingent. Organizing these partisans were a few Communist party members, deliberately left behind. By 1943, specialists, like radio operators, were frequently parachuted in or infiltrated into the occupied territory.

Military demographics of the German Army were odd. Despite the racial-purity objectives of the Nazis, manpower shortages in the German Army forced them to enlist many Soviet POWs. POWs faced with the choice of death from starvation or "volunteering" for the Germans chose the latter. Some conquered Soviet minorities, notably the Crimean Tartars and some Moslem people in the Caucasus Mountains with a long history of being ferocious fighters against Russia, were also accepted in large numbers as volunteers in the German Army. An entire Cossack corps fought on the side of the Germans. The turncoats numbered about one million. Their reliability was as good as any SS troop, for the simple reason that if captured by the Soviets, they were summarily shot as traitors. On the other side, German Field Marshal von Paulus, captured by the Soviets at Stalingrad, was signing appeals for German troops to surrender rather than continue fighting a lost war.

I was worried about my orders since the plan seemed crude and risky. But following orders saves one from too much thinking. Not having a choice adds a note of fatalism to any action. Vania had hopefully balanced the risks against the immediate need for radios and gave the order. Meanwhile, back in my green Organization Todt uniform, I was delivered to the railroad station in Berezovka, with the boxes. Only three freight cars were going to Nikolaev. The rest of the train was local. A Romanian conductor checked my ticket; otherwise no one bothered me.

When we reached the bridge over the river Bug, we met a train coming from the other direction and the freight cars were detached and hooked up to another locomotive. Except for the railroad men, I was the only passenger crossing the river. In half an hour, we were in Nikolaev. I was struggling with the boxes when MPs told me to halt. They then proceeded to scrutinize my papers. I expected the worst, but instead, they told me where I could borrow a cart for the boxes. Go figure. The radios and I were safely in Nikolaev, in one piece.

I was picked up at the station by a driver with a horse-drawn cart and transported out of town on a back road into the woods. The equipment and I were deposited in one of the partisan's better dugouts, which was damp and uncomfortable, at best. The next day, I trained and equipped another radio operator. My next order was to deliver the last radio to Dnepropetrovsk, 250 miles northeast of Nikolaev. "How?" I asked. "The same way," they said. "It worked before, *it will work again.*" I filled out my Travel Order and I was not sorry it was the last because I was sure they would find travel assignments for me until one time it wouldn't work again.

The train from Nikolaev was a troop transport, filled with replacements and wounded soldiers who were patched-up and heading back to the front. We sat on our packs or slept on the floor of the boxcar. The German soldiers were no longer the polished, proud warriors of earlier years. They looked dejected and tired. The replacement next to me must have been in his forties and he consumed inordinate amounts of bicarbonate of soda to steady his stomach. At night, someone played "Lilly Marlene" on the accordion. There was only one half-hearted ID check on the entire journey. However, when the train was at the station and I was getting some food from the field kitchen, I could see that the MPs did a much more thorough job on the trains going in the opposite direction. In fact, they dragged a uniformed man out of the train. Were they looking for deserters?

I underwent another routine ID check at the Dnepropetrovsk station without incident. My new "hosts" picked me up without delay. These partisans were located in a house in town and I actually had the comfort of a regular bed that night. They were a lot nicer and more appreciative than the Nikolaev lot, maybe because the assignment was not quite finished. Dnepropetrovsk was situated on the west bank of the river Dnepr and the radio operator I was sent to train was somewhere east of the river. He was deemed too valuable to cross the bridge. I was not. With my knowledge of German and my uniform, they counted on the fact that I could safely cross the bridge. I was to wait until the details of the drop-off were arranged.

Dnepropetrovsk was in turmoil. There were signs posted on the streets ordering the evacuation of the civilian population within two weeks, under the usual penalty of death. The Germans were now planning to withdraw to the defensive line of the river and they did not want to deal with civilians at their back.

German soldiers were chaotically emptying trucks filled with the personal belongings of the German civilian administration into the street. The German soldiers had requisitioned the trucks. A lot of yelling and hand waving accompanied this process but the guns won out. When the soldiers drove off, the locals quickly helped themselves to the booty.

In a couple of days, I got the "go" order. I divided the equipment into two loads so that I could fit each load into a backpack without weighing myself down. The bridge over the river was crowded with people and vehicles. The flow of locals to the west was allowed without any restrictions, but the flow of locals east, was blocked. Military personnel could move freely both ways. Since I had my uniform, I had no problem going east. In fact, I got across the river in comfort because I hitched a ride. The destination was the residence of the Rostovski family. It was a small hut, a mile's hike from the bridge. Rostovski and his wife were both in their sixties. I found the hut without any trouble, left the load, and hiked back across the bridge to Dnepropetrovsk. The next day, I delivered the rest of the equipment the same way. I had to wait at the Rostovski's a few more days until the radio operator showed up. My job was done and I headed back to Dnepropetrovsk.

To my great concern, the house in Dnepropetrovsk was deserted. Judging from the disarray, my hosts left in a great hurry. I walked around the block for a while and came back in an hour. There was still no sign of life. I collected my belongings that were undisturbed, just where I left them, hidden in the basement. I hiked back to the Rostovski's house on the east side of the river. They had no idea what happened and suggested that I stay with them until they found out. A few more days passed without any news. We could hear heavy artillery. The front line was getting closer. The Rostovskis said they were going to sit it out. I thought that this was very risky, in light of the German evacuation order. I was also concerned that the Germans might want to defend the bridgehead in front of

Dnepropetrovsk. I decided I would walk toward the sound of the artillery that was coming from the northeast. First, I got into my Kiev escape outfit: the green Organization Todt uniform and my backpack. The only thing left in my First Aid Kit was my ultimate weapon: my grandmother's diary. It was the evening of September 23, 1943, just a little over a year since I had escaped from the Ghetto. It might as well have been another lifetime.

Part 3

The Red Ally

Chapter 13

Crossing the Frontline

It was the middle of the night and I was completely alone – again. I was sitting in the smoldering kitchen of a burnt-out farmhouse. There was no use complaining since I had made the decision to leave the company of the Rostovskis. I had really welcomed the opportunity to cross the frontline. For so long, I had dreamed about finally escaping German rule. I longed to join the Allies and fight the Nazis. Yet I could not forget the Stalinist barbarism in the two years that I had spent under the Soviet occupation of Poland. Joining the Soviets was a reluctant decision. Still, the Soviets were the only allies within my reach and they were my only chance to even my personal score with the Nazis. The prevailing duality of feelings is best summarized by a remark Winston Churchill made after the German attack on the USSR and just before he allied himself with Stalin in 1941: "If Hitler attacked hell, I would put in a kind remark about the devil."

It is difficult for me to recall what I felt that evening in September, 1943, when I left the Rostovski residence and started walking to the northeast, along a dirt road leading to Podgorodnoye. I should have been scared. If I encountered a frontline soldier (of either side), it was likely that he would shoot first and ask questions later. That's why I picked a night crossing -- to evade everybody, both the Germans and the Russians in the immediate vicinity of the frontline. But as I walked further in my green German uniform, I should have wondered how I could surrender to the Soviets later, without getting shot.

These World War II events flood my mind like a black and white movie without the color of emotion. Maybe this emotional amnesia is a protective cocoon that I developed as part of an adjustment to post-war life. Maybe after being in constant danger, day in and day out, for such a long time, I learned to switch off feelings because they were interfering too much with my ability to survive.

There was quite a bit of military traffic on the road. The Germans were withdrawing toward the bridge at Dnepropetrovsk. This was dangerous for me since it increased my risk of running into MPs. I therefore turned off the road onto a narrow path that seemed to lead in the right direction. As I crept along in the fields, the evening quickly turned into night. I didn't need a compass to find my way to the frontline since the flashes of the artillery shells were as visible on the horizon as distant lightning, accompanied by the boom of explosions. Signaling flares of all different colors shot throughout the night sky.

I skirted a burning village with no signs of life. It was eerie. There was no activity, no lights, no people, no animals, and no sounds except for burning timbers and the howling of an abandoned dog. The inhabitants were either gone or in hiding. From where I was, all I could see were burning houses, a few discarded belongings, and strewn farming implements. Ordinary life ceased to exist here.

Earlier in the month, the Soviet front under General Rodion Malinovsky started a successful push west and by September 8th, the Soviets occupied Stalino, in the east Ukraine, and Mariupol, a port on the Sea of Azov.[8] On September 15, the commander of the German Army prevailed on Hitler to authorize a pullout behind the river Dnepr. Implementing the withdrawal, small regimental groups trudged on, often orienting themselves without maps and compasses, as best they could. During the day, the Germans fought detachments of Soviet tanks and motorized infantry that constantly harassed them. At night, the Germans moved back on foot along the railway lines and roads, and were sometimes harassed by the partisans. German rearguard defenses slowed down the enemy's progress, but the Red Army still moved west some 10 or 20 miles a day.

The Nazi standing order was a scorched earth policy: vacate the population, burn and destroy as much as possible. Withdrawing Germans followed this policy whenever time and opportunity allowed, delegating the job mostly to the turncoat Crimean Tatars who added rape, murder, and looting to the list. From a military point of view, German tactics avoided disaster. The troops were successfully withdrawn, including 200,000 wounded and hundreds of thousands of Ukrainian civilians beyond the river Dnepr.

I kept going towards the ever-louder sounds of fighting. Suddenly, a German soldier jumped from hiding and yelled: "*Hande hoch*" (hands up). I obliged. He saw my uniform. "What are you doing here," he barked. "I got lost from my unit" was my rehearsed answer. He lowered his gun; I dropped my hands. I looked at him and he seemed as frightened as I was, and obviously relieved that I was not a Russian. "I am lost myself," he admitted. "Did you see the third motorized battalion?" "No, I didn't," I said. "Man, be careful. Russians are only a few miles away" - was his parting advice. He left and I continued in the same direction, even faster, toward the front. I found some Soviet propaganda leaflets on the ground and picked one up to read.

The night was chilly and I needed some warmth and rest. I crept into an isolated, smoldering farmhouse and sat in the middle of what was once a kitchen. I was now surrounded by a four-sided fireplace created by the burning walls. A crib and what might have been carved wooden toys showed that a family had lived here with young children. I munched on some bread the Rostovskis had given me and read the leaflet. It advised the Germans to surrender and promised they would be treated well. "Ha, ha," I thought. Since I was very tired, I rested on the floor and dozed off.

After a while, I woke up and left the warmth of the house. Shell explosions were coming now from the left and the right. One came close enough that it made me hit the ground. I got up, dusted myself off, and continued walking toward the front. My adrenaline kept me going fast.

At dawn, I ran into three soldiers in a Soviet patrol. I raised my hands and yelled in Russian my rehearsed greeting: "Good to see you, comrades, I'm on your side." The patrol did not reciprocate in my friendly greeting. A soldier grunted and searched me for weapons. None was found and the Soviet patrol led me at gunpoint back to their unit. Their mission for the night was accomplished. They had caught a prisoner. I was escorted to the interrogation unit a few miles in the rear.

The frontline POW interrogation unit had already collected a few-dozen prisoners in German uniforms. We were herded together in a barbed-wire enclosure, surrounded by NKVD troops with their guns on the ready. Most prisoners looked tired and resigned. The captives were sitting or lying on the ground, covered with dirt, some with dirt mixed with blood. A preliminary interrogation held in a tent by two NKVD officers sorted out the Germans from the turncoats. The German majority was led on their way to a POW camp. Suspected Russian turncoats, namely seven Crimean Tatars whose unit formed the rearguard of the German withdrawal, were sorted out into another group. To my great dismay, in my Organization Todt uniform, and since I was not German, I was included in this group. We were marched off under heavy guard and herded into a musty dugout that must have been used by a farmer to store food. A guard with a submachine gun sat at the only door, facing us.

In about a half-hour, a "trial" began in a tent outside. A Russian lieutenant and a captain, both with a blue band on their caps indicating that they were NKVD officers, were the judge and the jury. (In general, the NKVD was the Russian equivalent to the Gestapo and specifically, they handled intelligence matters in the Red Army.) The first turncoat was dragged from the dugout. The trial lasted fifteen minutes and ended with a single shot likely to the back of the POW's head. On the Eastern front, one bullet was enough to do the job -- a firing squad was a luxury of the First World War that wasted ammunition and manpower.

My dugout companions were terrified but quiet, -- no wailing, no cries for mercy, and no last minute prayers. Another man was tried and shot and yet another, until I was the only one left. It was my turn. The interrogation started with routine questions by the captain.

"Name?" --

"Edwin Langberg." It took quite a bit of effort to reveal my true identity. I kept telling myself that it was safe now to be a Jew but my past experiences kept nagging: "BIG, DANGEROUS MISTAKE! Stick with assumed identity."

"Where are you from?"

"Drohobycz, Western Ukraine." (That is what the Soviets called the Polish territories occupied in 1939).

"Rank?"

"I am a civilian," I insisted.

"What are you doing in the uniform?"

"I used it to cross the front line."

I told them about my escape from the Ghetto in Drogobycz. I also told them about meeting Grisha in Odessa and how I delivered ten German radios to the Soviet partisans. My fifteen minutes were nearly up.

"Now, no more lies, Langberg or Strutinski or Hrutinski, or whatever your name is. Why were you sent here? What is your assignment?" the NKVD captain yelled. Was it now my turn for the one economical bullet? "The Germans gave me no assignment! I told you the truth," I yelled back, fear and hurt tearing at me.

I had not felt any safer telling the truth to the NKVD than I did before, telling lies to the Gestapo when I was Leslaw Hrutinski. The two NKVD officers looked at each other and I knew that my fate rested on the outcome of their silent exchange. "Should we shoot him now and save the bother or should we send him to the rear for further interrogation?" They pondered this for a few seconds that only seemed like an eternity. They decided to give me the benefit of the doubt. I was led back to the dugout, the only one left there to sleep out the night.

The next morning I was led under guard to a traffic checkpoint through a Ukrainian village, newly occupied by the Soviets. The villagers demonstrated their newly awakened political correctness by spitting and cursing at me. I tried to console myself that they were spitting at the German uniform I was wearing and not really at me. Not much consolation as I wiped my face.

The checkpoint was "manned" by a heavy-set female Russian soldier. I couldn't help noticing that the strap supporting her submachine gun interfered with her substantial breasts as she waived her flag in order to stop and start traffic for inspections. One look at her face and you would have no doubt that, big breasts or not, she would be good at using her gun. Her partner, another formidable female soldier, worked with her as a traffic controller. She checked the papers of the truck drivers and their passengers. Military personnel who needed transportation lined up next to the traffic checkpoint. Based on space and destination, the controller loaded new passengers onto trucks. This was quite a contrast to the strictly male German military.

When it was our turn, my guard and I were cleared onto an open truck. We rode for several hours. This was followed by an hour's march until we arrived at our destination, an NKVD interrogation camp. The heart of it was a large gloomy compound that was probably a jail in peacetime. I was locked up alone in a cell barely long enough for me to stretch out. I was given watery soup and a small piece of bread, not enough to keep hunger away but enough to avoid starvation. For the next two weeks, I would be awakened every night from a deep sleep for interrogation. For starters, the interrogator always began with the same scary question: What is the mission that the Germans gave you?

After a time, the interrogator asked me more questions about my background and about my involvement with the partisans. On this last subject, I could not be very helpful because my partisan "hosts" always made sure that I knew as little as possible. He also wanted to know more about the radio operators in Soviet uniforms. Here again, the only things that I could provide were first names, locations where I met them, and their personal descriptions.

One night during a wake-up interrogation, a Jewish NKVD interrogator addressed me in Yiddish. This did not go well for me. I could not very well explain to him, a communist, about my bourgeois upbringing and my father's contempt for Yiddish as the German jargon of the uneducated. I could understand Yiddish but I could only answer in German. "What kind of a Jewish name is Edwin, anyway?" he scornfully asked. He shook his head. I had flunked Yiddish 101. I told him that the Nazis had a different method of identifying Jews: circumcision. He was not convinced: "You could have been "handpicked" for this mission just because you happened to be circumcised." And so it went.

Then one blessed night, my interrogator hinted that the NKVD had contacted one of the radio operators I had mentioned and the operator confirmed my story. The next day, I was released from solitary confinement and transferred to a general population camp. Here, some one hundred people were housed in tents surrounded by a barbed-wire fence. The inmates were a mixed lot; there was even one Canadian among us. The common denominator was that we were not Germans, we were not locals, and we were captured during a Soviet advance under "suspicious" circumstances.

In the camp, a fellow named Ludwig befriended me; he was in his thirties, and also a Polish Jew. Ludwig had also lived under an assumed identity and worked for the Germans in the Ukraine. He was arrested when the Soviets liberated him during their offensive. He spoke fluent Yiddish and he had no problem convincing the NKVD of his Jewish identity. He offered to speak to his interrogator about me. This might have helped because in a couple of days, we were both released and ordered to go to a Soviet Army formation camp in the town of Stalino (now Donetsk) where we were going to be assigned to Red Army units.

I asked for permission to first go back to Dnepropetrovsk, some 100 miles west of where we were, and by now in Soviet hands. I wanted to pick up the hard-to-come-by belongings that I had left behind at the Rostovskis. The request was denied with a comment "*Zhiviy budiesh, nazhiviosh.*" (Loose translation that does not have the succinct ring of the original Russian: "If you survive, you will acquire new belongings.") A good motto for those times, maybe any times. For then, I borrowed a pair of underwear, socks, civilian pants, shirt, and sweater from Ludwig so I could get rid of my distinct and grungy Organization Todt uniform. In return, I carried Ludwig's heavy suitcase on our trip to the Red Army formation camp.

Chapter 14

Life in a Labor Battalion

The Red Army formation camp at Stalino was huge. Some 10,000 men were temporarily housed in large tents. We first reported to an Admissions tent. We were immediately sent to a delousing unit. The hot showers with plenty of medicated soap felt good. Next, there was a quick medical checkup: fifty naked men standing in a line and a woman doctor checking us for venereal disease. Then we were given Soviet uniforms. We each received a brownish shirt-like top worn on the outside, jodhpurs, Lend/Lease American-made laced boots, a long dirt-brown overcoat, and a hat with earflaps. We were also given one set of underclothing. One thing struck me as strange: the Red Army did not believe in socks. We wrapped our feet in cotton kerchiefs. Hereafter, every two weeks, we were marched to a shower for delousing. We would drop off our underwear and kerchiefs at the laundry and pick up clean underclothing at the other end, hoping that it would fit.

Finally, we were fed. We then received our tent assignment for a bunk. That night, I returned my civilian clothes to Ludwig who later managed to sell them to civilians who waited for such bargains from inductees.

The next day, I was interviewed for my assignment. Here, I quickly found that in the Soviet system, once you spent any time in enemy territory, even if the reason was totally outside your control and even if the Nazis oppressed you, you were labeled *suspicious*. For the suspicious, frontline assignments were rare since the Soviets worried that they might be tempted to desert. Most landed in labor battalions. This included both Ludwig and me, although we were assigned to different units. I was sorry to lose his company and, unfortunately, I heard later that he was blown up while clearing a minefield.

Our basic training, if you could call it that, lasted a few days. We were taught how to clean and shoot a rifle and how to stand at attention and salute. One of the pearls of wisdom that still sticks in my mind is that you were excused from jumping to attention while shaving. Considering that we did not have safety razors, this seemed like a good idea.

I was assigned to a labor battalion unit that was a repair shop. It centered on a captured, 100 kilowatt German diesel motor-generator that glistened under the mechanics' tender care. The generator provided light and powered all of our shop tools. It was now November and my unit was located in the Ukraine near Zaporozhie, some fifty miles to the south of where I crossed the frontline. The shop was at the end of the ramp approach to the railroad bridge over the Dnepr. The Germans had blown up the bridge in the middle of October during their withdrawal. This bridge was a part of the strategically important rail line to Crimea, still occupied by the Germans and Romanians and so the rebuilding had a very high priority.

Our job was to support the army engineers who were working on the bridge by repairing their vehicles and equipment and whatever else needed fixing. My unit consisted of a dozen mechanics and fifty or so worker ants like me who helped out, carted things around, and peeled potatoes. I was also part of the team that picked up defective equipment on the bridge and delivered repaired equipment from the shop.

The Germans were some 20 miles east of us, far enough away so that shelling was not a problem. We were only bombed once. At this point in the war, the Luftwaffe was not in great shape and the anti-aircraft artillery defense of the bridge was massive. In carting the equipment around, the main dangers to our unit were hidden anti-personnel mines, scattered for miles around the approaches to the bridge. We were losing several people a day until the mine clearing detachment finally cleared all mines from passageways.

The passageways were narrow, crisscrossed with building materials, and often covered with snow or ice. One such day, Serge, a fellow private, carried a motorized saw on the bridge. He slipped and fell into the freezing river. The current was swift and carried him some distance to a frozen ledge. He yelled and thrashed around until he managed to lift himself partially onto the ice. The three remaining members of our team ran to save Serge with a long wooden board. We got as close to him as the crumbling ice would allow. We then put the board on the ice.

Our corporal crawled on the board and grabbed Serge. As he pulled him onto the board, the weight of the two men caused the ice to break and the tip of the board submerged. We pulled the board as hard as we could and got the two of them on firm ice. Both were alive, but Serge was unable to move. The corporal shook violently. The two of us dragged Serge to the shore; the corporal followed unsteadily. This place on the shore was well outside the mine-free area, so there was not much chance of getting outside help. To make matters worse, the corporal soon collapsed. It took us quite a while, maybe 20 minutes, before we managed to drag Serge and the corporal to a heated hut. By that time, Serge was dead and the corporal died a few hours later.

Mines and construction accidents were deadly but there were also other more persistent problems. The further you were from the frontline, the smaller your food rations were. My rations were not as good as those in the prison in Odessa. Our sleeping accommodations consisted of straw on the floor of an unheated shack and our winter clothing was barely adequate. Perhaps a good indication of our condition was that there were no latrines. One just did one's business wherever one could find a frozen spot not already covered with shit. Long hours of work, cold, hunger, and filth were our daily routine.

For the son of a dental surgeon who would have his plaque removed before it ever formed, it was ironic that I had not owned a toothbrush since I crossed the frontline. My gums were bleeding profusely, whether from lack of hygiene or lack of vitamins, I do not know. One vivid memory of my time in the labor battalion had to do with my teeth. It was in January, 1944, just after New Year. There was deep snow on the ground. I awoke in the middle of the night with a terrible toothache and my jaw was swollen. In the morning, I reported sick and asked for a dentist. I thought, "Oh, if I could only find my father who I had hoped was also somewhere in the Soviet Army." A medic was the best that I could get.

The medic warned me that he had never pulled a molar, and he did not have any painkillers. I didn't have a choice, so I told him to go ahead. He yanked the tooth and broke the crown. He left the infected roots. As the day progressed, so did the pain and I was running a fever. My commanding officer gave me an extra ration of vodka and permission to walk to a nearby village, some five miles away to see if I could get some help there. I trudged through the snow, barely able to walk. The only medical person in the village was a versatile midwife, a stocky Ukrainian woman in her forties with a broad smile that uncovered her missing teeth. "No problem," she assured me. She had the right chisel for the roots and had been pulling teeth for years. She boiled water and got towels. I took a gulp of vodka and opened wide. She chiseled the roots one by one. The pain got so unbearable that I passed out. When I came to, she apologized. She said that she thought she was chiseling the last root but it was actually my jawbone.

By the end of January, our lot improved. The bridge job was complete and we were moved from the field and quartered in the town of Zaporozhie. Although food rations did not improve, our comfort level increased. We slept in heated houses that were converted into barracks. This was a great luxury in a cold winter. Our barracks were only a short walk from our repair shop, now located in an abandoned factory building. We even had an outhouse latrine.

New for me were the political education classes. The lectures were heavy handed and boring propaganda. I began to understand why the Soviets were so suspicious of anyone with even an iota of foreign exposure. One would have to be either totally isolated or a narrow-minded communist fanatic to believe that the USSR police state was a worker's paradise, or to believe in the many "blessings" that Stalin bestowed on its population. The lectures were similar to a religious gathering except that instead of quoting the bible, the *politruk* (political instructor) would quote the gospel according to Marx, Engels, Lenin, and Stalin. In the discussion of current events, every victory was the work of Stalin; every defeat was blamed on some shadowy and unspecified "class enemies."

In Zaporozhie, I was assigned to a sergeant named Nikita who was a shop foreman for things electrical. Although Nikita was a Ukrainian, we still spoke in Russian, the working language of the Red Army. He was an understanding, fine man in his early forties and we became quite friendly, friendly to the point where Nikita dared to tell me about the miserable life that he had had under the Stalin regime before the war. "If things don't change after the war, I will commit suicide," he once confessed.

I could readily appreciate his sentiment. When we were in the field, the extreme hardships were the result of war and therefore temporary. When we moved into town, our life was more like the typical life of a person in the Soviet Union: chronic deprivation, no freedom, and no hope. It was a most depressing thought that I should be stuck in the Soviet Union after the war. It was not hard to see by then that Stalin would be heralded as a great hero and things would never change for the better in his God-forsaken country or any other country that he managed to conquer. I had to remind myself that I crossed the frontline to fight Hitler and not to praise Stalin. But this was surely a depressing and unsatisfactory way to fight Hitler.

I should add that the majority of the population did not feel like Nikita. Propaganda, like advertising, dulls one's judgment and it works. Just as children like to hear the same story told over and over again, there is something soothing about hearing and believing in the same slogans. The state becomes a parental figure, taking care of everyone while doling out rewards and punishments. There is a need to endear oneself to the state. There is some comfort in believing you live and suffer for the glorious ideals of the communist state, and your life, as miserable as it may be, will lead to a glorious future, a sort of afterlife, when the whole world is communist.

Very few, after reading the obscure writings of Karl Marx, could critically understand what he had in mind. For those who did, the discrepancy between dismal reality and the glorious Marxist utopia resulting from the victory of communism would be explained by the excuse that the Soviet system was socialist and not yet communist. No one dared ponder the two basic flaws of Marxism. First, most people are motivated by self-interest and self-fulfillment and not by abstract ideals. Second, the ephemeral "dictatorship of the proletariat" quickly gravitates by natural political forces into just plain dictatorship, without any accountability for the murderous social, economic, and demographic policies of the government or the bloody paranoia of the ruler.

The chance of getting out of the labor battalion, a blessing if you will, came sooner than I could have hoped. In February, two months short of my 19th birthday, I was working on a tractor with a faulty ignition. I was outside of the shop when I saw a striking man in the uniform of a Polish officer walking down the street. I did a double take. He was not a mirage. He was real. His four-corner cap was unmistakable. I ran after him and caught up to him quickly because he walked with a decided limp. "Sir, are you a Polish officer?" I asked him in Polish, a bit short of breath from excitement.

"I am a Russian, but I am a captain in the Polish Army that is now being formed from former Polish citizens that live in the USSR. Are you Polish?" he asked in Russian. I stood tall with my shoulders back and said, "Yes, sir." "Then you should be eligible for a transfer to the Polish Army," he replied. "How do I do it?" I asked with curiosity, hope, and joy. He stopped walking at the house where he was quartered. "I am staying here on the second floor. Come see me this evening and ask for Captain Vladimir Rosnikov." "Yes, sir. Thank you, sir," I stammered. I'll see you at eight."

My excitement is hard to describe. I had hoped and prayed for a chance to get out from my present miserable situation. Was it possible that I could end up doing something more meaningful and purposeful in this war than being a half-starved zombie in a Soviet Labor Battalion?

Getting leave after working hours was not very hard. I arrived at Captain Rosnikov's promptly at eight. The captain was drunk and so was his good-looking landlady who was with him. Surprisingly, they greeted me as if I were a guest at a party. They offered me vodka and I readily accepted. I awkwardly sat there while the landlady and the captain were clearly having a good time. Quickly, she realized that three was not a good number and she suggested that she get her girlfriend to join us. The captain agreed and she left.

This was my chance. "Captain, how do I get to transfer to the Polish Army?" I blurted out. He lifted his drunken head and slurred, "Well, officially, there is an edict that you should be able to apply for a transfer. But between you and me this will be a waste of your time. I am here to pry loose a couple hundred Poles that applied for a transfer. But the sons of bitches at headquarters are giving me the run around." He cursed some more. "Isn't there anything that I can do? . . . *anything?*" I implored. I must have had tears in my eyes. I blabbed on and told him about my adventures with the partisans. This softened him, I guess. "Well, Edwin, you seem to be good at taking chances." "Oh, sir, I am a specialist with a long experience at taking chances." I bragged enthusiastically. Captain Rosnikov then reached into his pocket and awkwardly pulled out his travel orders and tickets. "I will be on the 2 p.m. Moscow train, the day after tomorrow, in compartment 27. I can't help you to get to the station, but if you meet me on the train ten minutes before departure, I will get you into the Polish Army. I hope you make it. I don't want to come back completely empty-handed." "It's a deal, sir." We drank to it.

The landlady came back with her girlfriend. Not a bad looking woman. We all got drunk and I was very late getting back to my unit. Fortunately, there was a sentry only at the shop, not at the house where we were quartered. My sergeant was sound asleep. No one cared that I arrived late.

I began to plot my escape with excitement. I knew if I were caught leaving, the Soviets would consider me a deserter. That did not stop me. I had to get out. I felt happy and exhilarated. I felt alive again. Little did I know that for me, danger was getting to be a needed antidote for depression. I was indeed hooked and this adrenaline dependence would linger long after the war was over.

Obtaining a leave during the working day was out of the question. Also, if I didn't show up at work or if I disappeared from work, they would be looking for me right away. I decided the only way to get off was sick leave. The only hitch was that I would really have to be sick. The medic was good at recognizing malingerers.

Luckily, some time ago during idle chatter, I had overheard one of the comrades saying that the best way to induce quick sickness was with *makhorka* extract. Soviet soldiers received a ration of tobacco. It was not regular tobacco leaf but was made from chopped tobacco stems. The Russians called it makhorka. They would roll it in a piece of newspaper and smoke it as a cigarette. You can imagine the foul taste and smell, but there was plenty of nicotine in makhorka to keep the addiction going. A soldier said that the best way to induce quick sickness was to boil the contents of a dozen makhorka cigarettes and to drink this concoction. I decided to try it.

Pretending that it was tea, I boiled and drank the foul-smelling, bitter-tasting brew at lunch the next day. I probably vomited most of it but enough remained in my system to cause violent trembling and heart palpitations. The medic was called and gave me a two-day sick leave. I was so weak I could barely walk across the street and crawl into my bunk. The next morning, I was glad I woke up at all. I stayed in my bunk until I felt stronger. By noon, I was dressed and headed for the railroad station with Sara's diary and a few rubles in my pocket. I arrived at the station in plenty of time so I waited in the toilet until 1:30 p.m. This was a very convenient place to hide since the diarrhea induced by my makhorka tea was still plaguing me. When the time came it was not hard to find the correct train and compartment. Much to my relief, Captain Rosnikov was there and was glad to see me.

"Do you have any travel documents for me, Captain?"--I whispered. He instructed, "When the travel document inspection comes, let me do the talking." "Remember, you don't speak any Russian. I will explain that a Polish officer always travels with his orderly and therefore my orders cover you." This was a complete fabrication, needless to say.

He fiddled in his bag and got a satchel with boot polish and a brush and gave it to me. "Concentrate on this," he said. I had gone through some brash railway capers, but this one seemed completely cockamamie. I looked carefully at Captain Rosnikov. He looked sober enough and had Soviet medals for bravery that gave him a look of competence. "Well," I consoled myself, "he survived to wear these medals, so he must be pretty lucky at taking chances." In any case, there was no alternative but to go along with my captain.

The compartment filled up. There was no room for me on a regular seat so I sat conspicuously on the floor on top of his case. The fifteen minutes at the railway station seemed long but the train started on time. I polished my captain's boots to justify my role, noticing in the process that his left foot was badly mangled. I realized that this injury explained his limp. I did my best to act like a serf sitting in front of my captain. He was clearly enjoying the game and the looks that he was getting from the other passengers, all Soviet officers, who were making envious jokes about him getting his shoes polished.

The Soviet military police came for inspection and Captain Rosnikov delivered his explanation of my presence, with complete nonchalance. I was astounded but the MPs bought it, saluted smartly, and moved on. In the evening, Captain Rosnikov struck up a conversation with a pleasant-looking nurse who was passing by in the corridor. He told me that he would be going to her compartment. "What if there's another inspection, Captain?", I whispered nervously. "Tell them that I am in the front of the train." "In Polish?" I wanted to know. "Yes, in Polish," he replied.

At least for a while, I had a regular seat. As I clung to the satchel with the brush and boot polish for company, I thought "what a nut!" I eventually dozed off. As I write it now let me add: "Thank you my captain for being a nut, for taking chances for me, and for getting me out of the labor battalion. I am proud to have polished your boots."

Chapter 15

Poles, Jews, and Uncle Joe

It may be hard to comprehend that my ticket out of the Red Army labor battalion would be provided by a Russian captain, a loyal communist as far as I knew, who proudly paraded himself down Soviet streets in a Polish uniform. Also hard to believe was that a Polish Army was forming in the USSR and seeking me as a recruit. It is difficult to make much sense of my story without digressions into the history of the stormy and perfidious relationship between Poland and Russia.

This enmity goes back centuries. Poland was partitioned among its neighbors Russia, Germany, and Austria at approximately the time of the American Revolution. For 100 years, Russia oppressed the Poles in their territory, trying to "russify" them and suppress Polish culture, language and the Catholic religion. Russia treated Jews with callous brutality. *Pogrom* -- an organized act of violence against Jews, looting their property, and raping their women -- is a Russian word. This is in strong contrast to the policies of Austria. The Austrian crown allowed all ethnic groups to live their own lives in its Polish province, Galicia, the home of my family.

After World War I, Poland was revived as an independent country by the Treaty of Versailles in June, 1919, but its eastern frontier was not firmly determined. Arguments about this frontier persisted for decades. At its historical prime in the 17th century, Poland was a commonwealth that included the Ukraine, Lithuania, and Byelorussia. Regaining this territory was the ambition of the new Polish leadership. After World War I however, its neighbors felt that Poland's boundary should be limited by the Polish-speaking majority -- not a well-defined line.

In 1919, while a civil war between the Reds and the Whites distracted Russia, the Poles occupied large parts of Lithuania, Byelorussia, and the Ukraine. The Bolsheviks saw the Polish advance as a threat to the survival of the Red revolution. A huge army was assembled and Poland was counterattacked. It was Lenin's plan to use this massive offensive not only to occupy Poland but also to come to the aid of German communists, thereby carrying the Red revolution to the heart of Europe. In the 1920 battle of Warsaw, the Poles decisively defeated the Soviets and the Soviet plan for widening the Red Revolution beyond Russia was thwarted. The Poles fondly refer to this battle as the Miracle on the Vistula. At the time, Stalin was already part of the Soviet leadership and he never forgot the humiliation of this defeat.

And so, in spite of the change from a Czarist Russia to Bolshevik rule, the old historical prejudices survived and became a self-fulfilling prophecy. The Soviets viewed the Poles as an aggressive, fanatically Catholic nation, dedicated to the overthrow of the Soviet system. The Poles viewed the Soviet Union, just like Czarist Russia, as a brutish archenemy, determined to squash their liberty and independence.

In 1917, at the beginning of the Bolshevik revolution, Jews were given full rights of citizenship for the first time in Russian history. Many Jews participated in the revolution; first among them was Leon Trotsky, heir apparent to Lenin. After Lenin's death, Stalin, with his usual cunning and brutality, took over. He managed to exile Trotsky and eventually had him assassinated. With suspicion that bordered on pathological, Stalin suspected Polish-Jewish communists of being Trotsky sympathizers. When Polish Communists, many of them of

Jewish descent, attended the 1938 International Communist Congress (Comintern) in Moscow, they were imprisoned and executed as unjustly suspected Trotskyites.

The lot of Jews in Poland between the world wars was a mixed one. Many Jews were quite successful in business, commerce, and the professions. Their economic success was very visible and was resented by many Poles. Eventually, the Poles instituted a system of quotas that severely restricted Jewish access to education. Of course, the masses of poor Jews who barely eked out a living were neither visible nor envied.

Between the wars, the State religion in Poland was Catholicism, and the Polish Catholic Church was notoriously anti-Semitic. Anti-Semitic diatribes of the Polish Primate, Cardinal Hlond, and the later sanctified Father Maximilian Kolbe are astonishing. Given Polish hostility, it is not surprising that Jews have not been as patriotic about Poland as the Poles. Jews tended to treat Poles with contempt and suspicion. Up until the middle of the 19th century, Jews were a nation within a nation, isolated not only by religion, but also by language, dress, culture, and traditions. Having witnessed Polish-Jewish relations first hand, I am painfully aware it is often too easy to speak of stereotypes, maybe representing the majority of a group, but this certainly was not the whole story. There were many genuine Polish-Jewish friendships. Many Jews died in defense of Poland, and later, under Nazi occupation, many Poles protected Jews at great peril to themselves.

When war broke out in 1939, fostered by the Nazi-Soviet Pact, Stalin swallowed up the eastern half of Poland. In a speech on October 31, Molotov stated the Soviet view as follows: "...one swift blow to Poland, first by the Germans and then by the Red Army, and nothing was left of this ugly bastard of the Versailles Treaty." In the Soviet "liberated" Polish territories, Stalin murdered both Polish and Jewish leadership -- including my uncle Elias, the lawyer and one-time head of the local Zionist organization. By the time of the outbreak of the Nazi-Soviet war in 1941, over a million former

Polish inhabitants were deported to the interior wilderness of the USSR, including my Uncle Elias' family.

After the defeat of Poland in 1939, Germany placed captured Polish soldiers in prisoner of war camps. Soviets also interned captured Polish officers in POW camps or Soviet jails. The Soviet NKVD surveyed Polish officers and picked a handful that were considered to be prospects for Communist "re-education." They were sent to the "villa of happiness" near Moscow, where under very comfortable circumstances, they were converted to the Soviet cause. Colonel Zygmunt Berling was one of these converts. He was later promoted to General and was in command of the Polish Army when I joined in 1944.

In 1939, some 43,000 Polish officers and men escaped into Romania and Hungary. Both countries were neutral at the time. From there, they made their way to France, determined to carry on with the war. With another 40,000 men recruited from the large Polish community in France, a Polish Army was formed there under the command of General Wladyslaw Sikorski. Sikorski not only served as commander-in-chief of the Polish Army, he was also head of the Polish government in exile. In 1940, the German Army attacked on the Western front. Within weeks, the French were in chaotic retreat and the British expeditionary forces in France were cut off and preparing to evacuate across the English Channel, through Dunkirk. Some Polish units were able to join in the evacuation and to board ships for Britain. Out of his army of 83,000, Sikorski was left with about 25,000 on British soil. The broken remains of the Polish regiments were then sent to Scotland where they prepared to defend the British east coast against an expected German invasion.

Winston Churchill had become the British Prime Minister and had formed a coalition government on the day that the German offensive began in 1940. He assured General Sikorski of his full support, ordering the heads of his armed forces to give the Poles assistance. The Polish government in exile reassembled in London. In August, 1940, the Battle of Britain opened, as the Germans began their air offensive against southern England and London. The offensive was intended to break the Royal Air Force and clear the way for a sea-borne invasion across the Channel. The one hundred and forty-five Polish pilots who fought in the RAF, in two Polish fighter squadrons, became a legend in wartime Britain for their ferocity, skill, and recklessness. They accounted for one in every six German aircraft shot down in the four months of the Battle of Britain, at a cost of 62 casualties.

By 1940, the British had broken the code of the German Enigma Coding Machine and organized a major effort to speed up the decoding of Nazi radio messages. This effort was started by a pre-war feat of the Polish military intelligence, aided by a group of brilliant young Polish mathematicians. They worked out the basis of the Enigma System, built prototype replicas of the machines, and passed all the results to the French and the British. This was probably the most important Polish contribution to the Allied victory since the Allies were then able to read secret German messages and to know enemy plans ahead of time.

On June 22, 1941, German armies stormed across the demarcation line that divided the German and Soviet occupation of Poland and attacked the Soviet Union. At once, Churchill offered unconditional support to Stalin. This put General Sikorski, as head of the Polish government, in a delicate position since he was dependent on British hospitality. He issued a statement rejoicing in the outbreak of hostilities between Poland's 1939 enemies, Germany and the Soviets. He suggested that any Polish-Soviet alliance should be conditioned on the abrogation of the Soviet claim to Polish territories annexed by the Soviets in 1939.

Another condition was the release of Poles in captivity within the USSR. The situation was very contentious because the Soviets refused to acknowledge the pre-1939 frontier. Combined British and Soviet pressure forced Sikorski to shelve the frontier problem. On July 30, 1941, a Polish-Soviet Agreement was signed in London. The pact merely stated that territorial changes under the 1939 Molotov - Ribbentrop Agreement were no longer valid. The agreement promised mutual support in the war, arranged for the formation of a Polish Army under the London government on Soviet soil, and declared that the Poles captive in the Soviet Union should receive amnesty-- although they had committed no crime save that of being Polish citizens. To comfort Sikorski, the British issued a declaration that stated that Britain did not recognize changes in Poland's borders after August, 1939.

Freeing Polish prisoners and deportees located in the Soviet Union well justified the Polish-Soviet Agreement in humanitarian terms. Slowly and reluctantly, the gates of the Siberian and Kazakhstan prison camps swung open, and hundreds of thousands of Poles and Polish Jews, soldiers, women, officials, priests, and even orphaned children, began to make their way towards the centers where the new Polish Army was being formed. Sadly, many were not released. Starvation and disease claimed many lives as they set out by rail, sled, river raft, and on foot. In the chaos of wartime, the Soviet authorities gave little assistance or food. My Uncle Elias' family was in a Kazakhstan labor camp when the news came of the Polish-Soviet Agreement. They were released and started their perilous journey to find the Polish Army. Many did not make it. There were so many people dying, the soldiers were assigned the job of burying the dead.

General Wladyslaw Anders was chosen by General Sikorski to be the army commander of the Polish forces in the USSR. Thus, the Polish Anders Army in the USSR had allegiance to Sikorski's London government. General Anders had first hand experience of Soviet hospitality: He had spent the previous two years in the NKVD Lubyanka prison in Moscow. He now set up his headquarters at Buzuluk, located between the Volga River and the Ural Mountains. My father had been mobilized into the Red Army, and I later learned that he eventually also made his way to the Anders Army at Buzuluk. By March 1942, Anders had 70,000 Polish soldiers. Strange and very ominous was the absence of the 15,000 former Polish POW officers, captured by the Soviets in 1939. Only a few hundred arrived.

Problems with slow release of the Polish prisoners, lack of food, and evasive answers about the missing Polish officers, coupled with his first hand impressions of the Soviet leaders, left Sikorski with no illusions about Soviet-Polish relations. Yet he remained convinced that there was no alternative to the pact with Stalin if Poland were to revive, victorious and independent after the war. But his problems only grew worse.

Early in 1942, Anders refused a Soviet request to send a division to the front on the plausible grounds that his men were under-armed and unfit. This refusal, later made much of by Soviet propaganda as evidence that the Anders Army was reluctant to fight the Nazis, covered a serious disagreement now emerging between Sikorski and Anders. Sikorski continued to stand by his agreement with Stalin that the Polish forces in the Soviet Union would fight on the Eastern front alongside the Red Army. The Polish forces under Anders were moved eastward to new camps near the Caspian Sea. The Soviet authorities cut their rations. A typhoid fever epidemic broke out. My father, whose fate I describe later, was on a medical team fighting this epidemic. Anders, whose distrust of Russians had grown even stronger, now pressed Sikorski to allow his forces to be evacuated to Iran that was under British control.

At first, Sikorski allowed Anders to evacuate only those he could not feed since Sikorski had three powerful reasons for keeping Polish troops in the Soviet Union. First, he would retain some leverage over Stalin. Second, the army would continue to act as a magnet and refuge for hundreds of thousands of Poles still missing. Third, above all, a free Polish Army under his command would help to liberate Poland from the east, thereby frustrating any Soviet attempt to bring Poland under Soviet domination. Unfortunately, Stalin understood this last reason perfectly. Stalin decided this alien presence on his own soil was more trouble than it was worth. Since the German thrust at Moscow had been beaten off in December, 1941, Stalin's military situation was no longer desperate. Stalin began to encourage Anders to leave Soviet soil.

Meanwhile in London, Churchill - now desperate for troops to stem the German offensive against Egypt that began under General Rommel in June 1942 - also started pushing the Polish government to let Anders leave Russia. Sikorski was in no position to defy this combined pressure. In August, 1942, ships carrying Polish troops set out across the Caspian Sea for the Iranian shore.

In all, Anders was able to lead some 115,000 soldiers and civilians, former Polish citizens, out of the Soviet Union. Unfortunately, anti-Semitism was rampant in the Anders Army, fueled by the Polish stereotype that Jews welcomed the Soviet invasion in 1939. This was a particularly painful insult to those Jews who suffered greatly under the Soviets. A great source of friction was the presence of two diverse groups: on one hand, mostly Polish prisoners of war and deportees, and on the other, mostly Jewish refugees who voluntarily fled Soviet territory ahead of the German invasion. The common oppression of both Poles and Jews by the Soviets should have, but did not, heal the friction.

At the last moment, the Soviets objected to the departure of anyone who had Polish citizenship but not Polish nationality - which meant the Jews. General Anders, to his credit, beat off this Soviet objection thus undoubtedly saving many Jewish lives. Among the evacuees were the members of my uncle Elias' family and Menachem Begin, the future leader of Israel. My father was one who did not make it. He died in a typhoid fever epidemic. I did not find this out until four years later.

In the safety of Iran, the British gave the refugees sufficient food and clothing to live. The troops were issued new weapons. But not all Poles were released, and even if released, not all could make it to the Anders Army. So about a million former Polish citizens remained in the Soviet Union with little leverage for freedom. Many Poles saw the evacuation to Iran as divine intervention, like a flight from Babylonian captivity. But for Sikorski, it was his worst diplomatic defeat and a political calamity. All of his efforts to preserve at least a working relationship with the Soviet Union were about to be smashed apart.

On April 13, 1943, German radio announced the discovery of mass graves near the village of Katyn, in the district of Smolensk. Katyn was a Soviet territory but the Nazis had occupied it since the summer of 1941. In the graves lay bodies of Polish officers with their hands tied behind their backs and their skulls shattered by pistol-shots from behind. The first Nazi broadcast reported 10,000 bodies. In fact, some 4,300 bodies were actually dug up.

The Germans proclaimed that the Polish officers had been murdered by the Soviets in 1940, before the German-Soviet war even started. At first, the Poles hesitated. They instinctively rejected murder charges made by mass murderers like the Nazis. The Poles could see the deadly diplomatic trap into which the Nazi propaganda intended to push them. They found it hard to believe that even the Russians could have committed a crime so revolting.

But the evidence was too strong. Papers found on the bodies, the condition of the bodies, and the vegetation growth above them, left little room for doubt. These were the Polish Officer prisoners from the Soviet camps that were established in 1939. They had been shot between April and early June, 1940. Now, the Poles remembered all of their 1941 and 1942 inquiries about the missing 15,000, whose letters had stopped so suddenly in the spring of 1940. They remembered Stalin's strange, evasive answers to Sikorski and Anders about the POWs: "They escaped to Manchuria," or just, "Things sometimes happen . . ."

The Soviet NKVD had indeed shot the Polish officers in Katyn. The order, released a half-century later by Russian President Boris Yeltsin, had been signed by Stalin and rubber-stamped by the rest of the Politburo. No trace has ever been found of the other 5,000 missing POW Polish officers in the Kozielsk special camp, or the 4,000 officers in the Starobelsk camp, or the 6,500 prisoners at Ostashkov. POW camps were "wound up" in April 1940. After that, there was only silence and darkness. One account circulated years later in the gulags said that the Poles who were not shot in Katyn, were locked inside barges deliberately sunk in the White Sea. For

Stalin, our ally in the fight for freedom and democracy, this would have been a small affair compared to some of his other slaughters.

Two days after the German announcement about Katyn, Radio Moscow announced it was the Germans who had committed the atrocity in 1941, after capturing Smolensk. The Polish government, in spite of Churchill's warnings to Sikorski, demanded a Katyn inquiry by the International Red Cross. For the first time, an open split had appeared in the anti-Hitler coalition. The German propaganda machine rejoiced over its triumph. As a result, on April 24, 1943, the Soviet Union broke off diplomatic relations with the Polish government in London, accusing it of a treacherous blow to the USSR and of siding with Hitler.

In the aftermath of the Katyn affair, while the British still reproached the Poles for provoking a breach in the alliance, Sikorski flew to the Middle East. He met General Anders and visited his troops, now in Iraq and about to be formed into the Second Polish Corps to take part in the invasion of Italy. Sikorski set off for home, making a landing at Gibraltar. The next day, on July 4, 1943, his aircraft took off from the Gibraltar airfield. The plane lost altitude at once and crashed into the sea. All but the severely injured Czech pilot died. He claimed that the elevator controls of his Liberator aircraft jammed and caused the catastrophe.

It is worth noting that when Sikorski was at Gibraltar, the British Governor General Mason McFarlane was hosting the Soviet ambassador to Britain, Ivan Maiski and his entourage, who were on their way to Russia. McFarlane had managed to keep the two groups apart. More importantly perhaps, Kim Philby, a high official in British Military Intelligence, was also at Gibraltar. Many years later, he was unmasked as a Soviet spy. He fled to the Soviet Union in 1963 and died in Moscow in 1988. Sikorski's plane may have been poorly guarded; indeed, by at least one account, the guards were asleep on the night of July 3. Thus, sabotage was possible. In 1993, Polish experts conducted a computerized investigation, concluding the crash could not have been an accident. A British inquiry at the time found no traces of sabotage in the aircraft wreck, concluding that a rudder had probably failed. Was this wartime whitewash needed to keep the alliance together?

The death of Sikorski was both tragic and disastrous to the cause of Polish independence. Upright, austere, and not without arrogance, Sikorski possessed a heroic authority that held the hostile factions together. Only he would have been capable of enacting a reasonable, equitable alliance with the Soviets that could have saved some semblance of Polish independence after the war.

Stalin had certainly benefited from Sikorski's loss because Stalin now had, in effect, a free hand in shaping the future of Poland through a new Polish Army. Soviet diplomatic relations with the Polish Government were broken off, yet Western aid kept flowing. Stalin was thus careful and played his political Polish diplomatic game with care. One of his main problems with his Western Allies was the future of the Polish State. Stalin's objective now was to have another Polish Army, totally dependent on the Soviets. There were still hundreds of thousands of Polish citizens in the USSR to form a potential pool for the newly created army.

Stalin moved rapidly to set up this new Polish Army of his own. In May, 1943, the nucleus of a Polish Army under Soviet command was started at a formation camp in Sielcy (a village on the river Oka near the town of Ryazan) some 150 miles southeast of Moscow. The army was led by General Zygmunt Berling, one of the Polish POW officers "re-educated" in Moscow's villa of happiness by the Soviet Communists after the defeat of Poland in 1939. His second-in-command was General Karol Swierczewski who had fought as the illustrious "General Walter" in the Spanish Civil War. In his eagerness to have his Polish Army, Stalin even authorized transfers of many officers and other specialists from the Red Army. Many were ethnic Russians who had no previous connection with Poland whatsoever, just like my captain. Stalin's primary objective was political: Soviet control of Poland. The Berling Army saw little action on the front lines until the Polish territory was liberated from the Germans.

The political indoctrination of the new Berling Army came from the Union of Polish Patriots (ZPP), a grouping of pro-Soviet Poles headed by Wanda Wasilewska. She was a pre-war leftist writer who found herself under Soviet rule and quickly became Stalin's favored Polish representative. She was a member of the Supreme Soviet and a political Commissar in the Red Army. A declaration prepared by the ZPP stated that a liberated Poland must have "just borders" in the east. This meant agreeing to the Soviet annexation of Poland's eastern territories. In the west, there must be a return to the "old Polish lands" on the Oder and Baltic. This meant forcible displacement of Germans from lands they occupied for centuries and replacing them with Poles. The agricultural structure would be reformed, the peasants would receive free land, and the nation would see "Poland liberated from the rule of landowners, cartel barons, usurious bankers, and speculators." [13] However, the most important point of the Declaration, confirming what was to happen in the near future, was the statement that "the only wise policy . . . is an alliance with the USSR."

Joining Stalin's new Polish Berling Army was the only hope for many Poles to get out of the USSR after the war. It was not long before tens of thousands began to pour into the Berling Army camp. The volunteers were Polish deportees and those who voluntarily moved east to avoid German occupation. In addition, there was an official edict, though often ignored, to transfer former Polish citizens kept as "politically suspect" in the Red Army labor battalions.

I was one of them.

Chapter 16

Promotion to Private

Fortunately, there were no inspections while my captain was romancing the nurse on the train. I dozed off in his seat. Thankfully, by the next morning's inspection, he was back. This time he didn't even explain to the MPs about my job polishing his boots. He just said, "He's with me." I began to suspect his travel orders might cover the possibility of bringing back soldiers with him. I sincerely hoped so; I did not want my survival to depend on the captain's spinning fantastic stories each time we had an inspection. He might have been able to get away with it once, but our journey was going to be a very long one.

We traveled on the Moscow train some five hundred miles north. During the journey, my captain mostly talked to the other Soviet officers in the compartment. I kept a low profile and a respectful distance. Everyone carried his own rations and my captain shared his U.S. lend-lease canned food with me. We went from Zaporozhie to Kharkov, still in the Soviet Ukraine, and then through Kursk to Tula in Soviet Russia. Most of the bridges we crossed were just barely patched up. All of the railroad stations were in ruin. In some areas, notably around Kursk, hardly a house or a tree was left standing.

We arrived at Tula in the afternoon, two days after our journey began, late in February 1944. We left the train quickly. My captain and I hitched a 150-mile ride on a truck to Ryazan, courtesy of the ever-present female Red Army traffic controllers. Now that we were off the train, the captain became a lot less formal. We talked quite a bit about my experiences under the Germans. From Ryazan, it was only a short ride to the formation camp of the Berling Army in Sielcy, 150 miles southeast of Moscow. It was night when at last we safely arrived.

The next morning I was awakened early. My captain brought me in front of his superior, a heavily decorated major. My captain left, and that was the last I ever saw of him. I never even had a chance to properly thank him.

The major was in his forties and built like a wrestler. He spoke Polish, but from his accent and demeanor I could guess he was born and raised in the USSR. I stood very straight in front of him. "Captain Rosnikov told me some of your story," he said. "But how exactly did you get out of the labor battalion?" I told him everything, even about the makhorka extract. He huffed a bit and hit the table hard: "Don't you know that desertion from the Red Army is a capital offense, young man?" he yelled. "Oh God," I thought, and my knees began to shake. "Not another jail-in-Odessa trick."

But this was not the case. The outburst was just the major's little joke to make sure I was not getting too big for my britches. He laughed in delight and slapped me on the back. I feigned a chuckle. "We need men like you," he said. "Just for that escape, you can pick your branch of service. If I were in your shoes, I would go for military intelligence. You know languages. You have valuable experience. You seem to have a knack for it. I have some influence in that branch and can guarantee you a commission in a few months," he assured me.

I saw myself, with horror, interviewing some terrified POW and deciding whether he should be shot now or sentenced to a slow death in a Soviet POW camp. "Sir, if you don't mind, I would rather be a pilot," I pleaded.

"You may be missing a good chance. It's an honor to be in intelligence," he assured me. "Are you sure?" he tried again. "Yes, sir, I am sure." This time I sounded as determined as I could, hoping he wouldn't just order me into military intelligence. "I should have known," grunted the major, sorry now that he had given me a choice, and then he added with a frown, "Why is it that every red-blooded 19 year old wants to be a pilot?"

In retrospect, the major was right. I would have attained a much higher rank had I chosen military intelligence. Yet, my on-the-spot decision was one of the best decisions I ever made. Chances were good that the prisoners whose fate I would have had to decide would have not been Germans, but Poles who belonged to Armia Krajowa (the Homeland Army), a well-organized Polish underground controlled by the Polish government in London. I now realize this decision saved my soul.

The interview was over. The major barked some instructions to a sergeant in the front office, and that is how I got started on my career in the Polish Army. Later, when I filled out my personnel questionnaire, I remembered the trouble I got myself into after crossing the frontline with my Jewish or German-sounding name. This time, I opted for a pragmatic solution. For my last name, I gave a hyphenated Dlugosz-Langberg. Dlugosz (dwoo-gosh) in Polish and Langberg in German both contained the word "long" and so, Dlugosz was in a way a Polanized version of Langberg. The name Dlugosz, in everyday use, unlike Langberg, would not raise questions.

It was exciting to see the Polish flag fly over the camp and to hear the Polish national anthem played again. The salute, the uniforms, and the insignia worn resembled those of the pre-war Polish Army. The Polish eagle, without the pre-war crown, was worn on our square caps. The rest of the induction process was not too different from the one I went through at the Red Army formation camp in Stalino: a shower and delousing; a medical check up; and the issue of a Polish uniform and pack. I thought I looked quite smart in my new Polish uniform - - but I had no one to brag to.

Everything was designed to maintain an outward Polish appearance in the camp. I was even told a priest was kidnapped by Soviet partisans on Polish territory and smuggled through the frontline. He was delivered to Sielcy in order to say mass on Sundays, to make the Polish men feel at home. But even though everything was done to color the camp Polish, it still seemed Soviet drab around the edges. The uniforms were not worn with the same panache, the faces of the soldiers showed the shadows of the Gulags, and the officers spoke in Russian.

At night, I slept peacefully for the first time since the excitement of meeting my captain. Our large tent housed many soldiers. It was noisy and aromatic, but it was the Polish Army. No more Russian labor battalions for me. The next morning, I was issued a service ID book and travel orders for the Polish First (and only) Air Squadron, now being formed in Grigoryevskoye. The major had kept his word.

I had a good trip from Sielcy to Grigoryevskoye through Moscow and Yaroslavl. For me, the trip was very unusual and luxurious since I was now traveling with my own honest-to-goodness travel documents and my almost real name. I had no worries about MPs and their inspections. I was now Private Edwin Dlugosz-Langberg and on my way. I had few possessions, but I still had Sara's diary with me, the only relic of my old First Aid Kit. I was in the real army now, and I was finally going to fight for the cause. Sielcy was about 150 miles southeast of Moscow. The airfield at Grigoryevskoye was another 400 miles northeast of Moscow, so I traveled through the Soviet capital. When I arrived in Moscow, I had a couple of hours to pass between trains, so I rode the Moscow subways, which was all the sightseeing I could afford to do considering my finances and limited time. I had never been on a subway. The Moscow Metro stations looked like marble palaces, unlike anything I had ever seen. The Metro was Stalin's pet project and construction started in the early 1930s and never stopped. It didn't stop during the forced collectivization, when millions of people died of starvation in the Ukraine, nor during Stalin's purges that consumed the cream of his party and army. Construction didn't even stop during World War II when I was there. All of the marble, the chandeliers, sculptures, and murals in the Metro are a lasting, if macabre, monument to Stalin.

In a few days, I finally arrived at the Warszawa (Warsaw) Squadron training camp at Grigoryevskoye. The camp was set in bucolic surroundings, a countryside covered with birch woods and meadows. There were no signs of the destruction of war since the Germans never got that far east. The camp was relatively small; there were only a few hundred people. The squadron's camouflaged planes were parked in the open, to the side of a grass landing strip. The command post, barracks, mess hall, and support shops were all located nearby.

Captain Czeslaw Kozlowski, an ethnically Polish pilot born and raised in the USSR, commanded the squadron. He had been transferred from the Red Army. The absence of experienced pre-war Polish pilots and crews was not surprising. Most of the Polish Air Force had flown to England after the defeat of Poland in 1939. Those who remained later left Russia with General Anders. Our personnel comprised an even mixture of transferees from the Red Army and Polish trainees. Except for a few ethnic Poles born in the USSR, the transferees had nothing to do with Poland and of course, did not speak Polish. Russian was the working language of the squadron. The unit trained Polish airmen but, at the time when I joined, it was a long stretch to see it as a Polish unit.

On admission to the squadron, I was re-equipped. I received overalls for duty and a black uniform for more formal wear, with a round cap fashioned on the prewar Polish Air Force. This time, I was even issued socks rather than Russian handkerchief wraps. I knew then I was on my way back to civilization. Our accommodations by war standards were comfortable, and our food rations were adequate. Most meals consisted of soup and bread. The amount of bread one received was based on the importance of your unit's work assignment. For the first time since crossing the frontline, I brushed my teeth again.

Unfortunately, by the spring of 1944, the pilot training admission program was closed to any new trainees, with or without shiny teeth. The pilot class had been in training for almost six months. Plans for new squadrons had not yet jelled. Needless to say, this was a huge disappointment to me. When my assignment officer found out about my adventures with the partisans and the German radios, he decided radio mechanic's training was an ideal spot for me.

Our unit was called a hunter squadron. We had nine Yak-1 fighter planes and a few UT-2 double-seater bi-planes, used mostly for training. All of these planes were early World War II vintage. Not exactly state of the art, but still battle worthy.

The Yak-1 was named after its designer, Aleksander Yakovlev. It was a single-pilot low-wing monoplane with lines similar to the British Spitfire and German Messerschmitt 109. It was light in weight and high in power. Its cannon was located between the cylinder banks, firing through the propeller shaft. It had two synchronized machine guns also firing through the propeller arc. For infantry support operation, six 82-mm rockets could be slung beneath the wings. Its maximum speed was 370 mph.

There was no formal radio mechanic training, even though the job was demanding. I was trained by Nikolay, a 20-year-old Russian Red Army NCO transferee. I really liked Nikolay. He was bright and quite good at his job and he gave me books on electricity and radios to read. For good measure, I had to go though marching drills, fitness training, rifle cleaning, and target practice. Nikolay was the first one to tell me about the existence of radar, which at the time was a big secret. Radar seemed like a miracle of ingenuity to me. Soviet-made radios, like most radios of the vacuum-tube age, failed quite often, so we had plenty of opportunity for on-the-job training. I got along quite well with the other Russians in our unit. My feelings for Stalin did not interfere with my relationships with them and I learned quite a bit. I became a radio mechanic and a corporal on July 28, 1944, and eventually a sergeant on May 1, 1945.

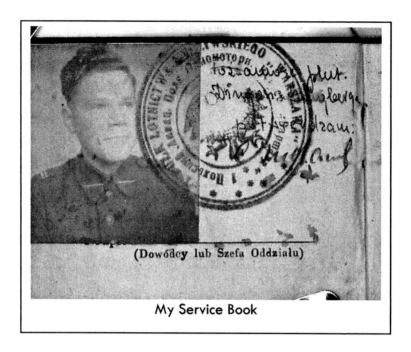

(Dowódcy lub Szefa Oddziału)

My Service Book

My elevated rank entitled me to new duties; one included being in charge of kitchen patrol (KP). My main duty was to make sure food was not stolen. Kitchen workers consisted mostly of local women, no great beauties, but the only women around the camp. They peeled potatoes, mixed them with other ingredients, and made a daily chowder in a big vat. On my first day in charge of KP, after the meal was completed, the women washed the utensils and cleaned up. Before I could say anything, the women stripped off their underclothes and washed them in the soup vat, now full of clean boiling water. They did not miss the opportunity to kid me mercilessly about my reaction. The next day at lunch, Nikolay commented to me that the soup had an unusual flavor.

In addition to the military training, we also had to go through a dull course of political indoctrination. Our two education officers were communists, ethnic Poles born in Poland, supplied by the Wanda Wasilewska's Union of Polish Patriots. I had come to the squadron freely to serve and fight. I believed in the necessity of the struggle against Germany and there was no disagreement on this point. Any admission by the communists of the wrongs done by the Soviets in the occupation of Poland during 1939-1941 -- or any indication the system would change from a police state -- might have convinced me communism had its good side. However, the Polish communists never presented their case this way.

In a country of deceit and terror, they could not and dared not admit to any faults in the Stalinist policies, past, present, or future. The constant praises of Stalin were painfully boring to me. Yet, Stalin stared at me with his beady eyes from the ever-present posters and seemed to say: "You can run from me, but you can't hide, Langberg!" I was afraid of him. Maybe instilling fear of the omnipresent and omnipotent Stalin was just as valuable for the propagandists as making us love him. Maybe indoctrination was not so stupid.

In August, 1944, just as the Soviets reached what they recognized as Polish territory, the Berling Army was taken out of its cradle and our unit, among others, was moved to the frontline.

Chapter 17

Squadron Warszawa

It was late July, 1944. Except for the planes and the pilots who flew them, the entire Squadron Warszawa was loaded into boxcars headed for the frontline in Poland. This included ground crewman, Corporal Edwin Dlugosz-Langberg.

Our squadron had been declared combat ready and we became officially part of the First Polish Berling Army. Of course, most of us were young and eager to see some action, or *"ili grud v ordenach ili golova v kustach"* -- which means "a chest full of decorations or my head in the bushes," as we proudly said in Russian.

So, with high hopes and some straw on the floor for bedding, the Squadron Warszawa spent ten days on a train being transported from the middle of Russia into Poland. All I can say is that we had plenty of leisure time and there were only two dominant subjects of conversation: food and women. If we were hungry, it was food. If we were full, it was women. We didn't speculate as to what fighting on the frontline would be like. We thought we were ready for action.

Since it was July, it was hot on the train. There was nothing to complain about, although a good shower at a bania would certainly have improved the aroma. Every once in a while, the train stopped to change crews or locomotives, and we would get off to stretch our legs and talk to the locals. A flood of memories was triggered when we crossed into Poland and I heard locals speak Polish again. Thoughts of my father were never very far from my mind.

On the tenth day, we disembarked at the Dys Airfield near Lublin, some 200 miles southeast of Warsaw and 30 miles from the nearest frontline. Strangely enough, the most vivid thing I remember about my first day back on Polish soil is a cherry tree. It was growing in an orchard nearby. I offered to buy some cherries from the farmer. "Just climb the tree and help yourself," he said. *So I did.* I gorged myself until I was ready to drop off, like a leach off a fat belly. My vitamin-starved body felt very grateful, and with red hands and a very red tongue I had a good nap in the warm Polish summer sun. To this day, I cherish cherries.

Radio Ground Crew: I am seated on left and Nikolay is standing on the right.

In addition to our squadron of Yak-1's, and right next to us at the Dys Airfield, was a squadron of IL-2 Shturmovik (attacker) aircraft that served for close infantry support. The IL-2 crew consisted of the pilot and a rear gunner who operated an 8-mm anti-aircraft machine gun. The Shturmovik had a 7-mm armor-plate backbone designed to protect the pilot and all of the critical plane components against ground fire. The price of the heavy armor was that the IL-2 was rather slow, only about 280 mph, making it easy prey for enemy fighters. Nicolay and the three mechanics under him (myself included) serviced the radios on both the Yak-1 and IL-2's.

Each day of that first week, we worked hard getting the squadron ready for battle. On the first Sunday morning, our political officer told us to spruce up and put on our best uniforms. There were no exceptions other than those on sentry duty. We figured that someone important would be reviewing the troops before battle. Instead, we were marched to a local Catholic Church for mass. Apparently, one of the jobs of the Berling Army in Poland was to convince the local population we were as Polish as Uncle Joe could make us.

As I mentioned before, the majority of our unit was Russian-born and raised in the USSR. They had never been to a church. Of the Polish-speaking contingent, many were Jews who also had never been inside a Catholic Church. But an order was an order, and we listened up. The logistical problem was how to teach "heathens" proper church etiquette. Our political officer solved the problem: he told all those who had been to a Catholic Church before to sit in the aisle seats. The rest were instructed to watch the person on the aisle for a cue what to do. Of course, Leslaw Strutinski knew which knee was used for genuflecting, but I kept my mouth shut. We all filed in and took our seats.

Mayhem prevailed. When an aisle-seat soldier stood before kneeling, the rest of the men stood. Unfortunately, some of them failed to notice the kneeling and remained standing. Huge waves of men were moving from a sitting to a standing and then to a kneeling position at all times. It looked like a wave at a football game. The priest was puzzled by the continuous movement of men behind him and the altar boys could not stop giggling. Needless to say, the locals were amused and chuckled among themselves. When the priest turned with relief to give the final blessing, it seemed every soldier did something different, with awkward clumsiness. When the priest motioned with his hand, "In the name of the Father, and of the Son, and of the Holy Ghost," some soldiers put their hats on and some finally took their hats off; some genuflected on whatever knee, and some blessed themselves with their right hand, and some with their left, in every possible combination of the cross from the forehead, the chest and both shoulders. The charade was not repeated -- we were never ordered to Mass again. The locals may not have been impressed with the new Polish Army, but they sure had a good laugh.

The Soviets had formed a "Polish Committee of National Liberation" in Lublin, a communist-dominated provisional government. We were harangued daily on the virtues of the communists, as contrasted with the "reactionary evil" of the Polish government in London. The Homeland Army, loyal to the government in London, was now declared an enemy. This was a new and dark development; the sudden shift from ally to enemy was hard to digest. I could sense a rising tension and a premonition that something was going on around us.

The original plan of the Homeland Army was to rise up in different parts of the country, just as the Germans were pulling out. The Homeland Army would then cooperate with the Red Army. So, as the Red Army advanced westward, the Homeland Army units came out into the open and helped the Soviets fight the Germans. The Red Army accepted their cooperation, but there was a hitch. On each occasion, the NKVD arrested the officers and ordered the men of the Homeland Army to join the Polish Berling Army. The officers who refused were either shot or deported to Russia, while the rank and file were forcibly conscripted. Naturally, when word got out, the Homeland Army units resisted and retreated westward, still hoping at some point to make a stand that would provide the London government with a means to influence the fate of Poland.

The trump card in the political game was Warsaw. Polish leaders assumed that if the Homeland Army freed Warsaw before the Red Army entered, the Soviets would have to recognize them. The Soviets would then have to give the London government some voice in deciding an independent future for Poland.

The new Polish Prime Minister Stanislaus Mikolajczyk, who had succeeded General Sikorski after his untimely death in Gibraltar, traveled from London to Moscow. He wanted military cooperation with Stalin. He told Stalin the Homeland Army in Warsaw would rise against the Germans. Stalin was skeptical, but hinted the Red Army too would enter the city soon. Both the Polish government in London and the Homeland Army *believed Stalin*. After all, Warsaw was the key road and rail center between Moscow and Berlin. The Russians were then expected to drive full speed for the German capital and get there before their Western Allies.

So, the move was on. The London government authorized the Homeland Army commander in Warsaw to choose the moment for the uprising. Meanwhile, the Germans demanded 100,000 Poles report for work on fortifications on August 1. The Homeland Army had to make their move before they would lose their pool of soldiers. At the same time, Russian guns could be heard east of the Vistula, the river flowing through Warsaw, and sightings of Russian tanks were reported. Soviet radio stations were calling on the people of Warsaw to rise and help the Red Army. General Tadeusz Bor-Komorowski of the Home Army chose the afternoon of July 31 for the Polish uprising against the Germans. Our unit was located within flying distance of Warsaw and with great anticipation, we waited to take part in the battle.

When the Warsaw uprising broke out, the German garrison numbered 15,000. It was quickly reinforced by a Cossack regiment known as the Vlasov Army, a German SS Brigade of a thousand freed criminals, and the mostly Ukrainian, Kaminsky SS Brigade. The atrocities perpetrated against civilians and the lack of discipline in the brigade even shocked the commanding German SS general who had

Kaminsky shot. Tanks, armored cars, heavy artillery and planes supported the German troops.

On the other side, the Homeland Army had about 40,000 poorly armed soldiers. Their goal was to seize the main roads, bridges, and center of the city. They expected the fighting to last only a few days, after which, they would hand over the city to the Soviets.

**Dugout on the Airfield in Lublin.
On the right is my Commanding Officer**

Of course, Stalin realized the political implications of the Red Army entering a Warsaw already liberated by the Homeland Army. He stopped the Soviet advance in its tracks. The Soviet radios were silent on the uprising. Our squadron, named after the city, was within easy flying range of Warsaw. Our air support could have made a decisive difference -- and we waited for orders that never came.

Stalin might have been willing to help the Warsaw insurgents if Prime Minister Mikolajczyk had accepted Stalin's territorial demands: He wanted the prime minister to cede the eastern half of Poland to the USSR and merge his government with the communist-dominated Polish Committee of National Liberation. Mikolajczyk wouldn't. He knew the uprising had the support of the West and he didn't think Stalin would risk antagonizing his Allies by sacrificing the city. He didn't know Stalin very well.

When Mikolajczyk departed Moscow on August 9, Stalin made up his mind. He refused to occupy Warsaw and instead let the Germans accomplish his objective of destroying the Homeland Army. The Soviet press -- and consequently, the Lublin Polish press -- and radio condemned the uprising as a "political trick." They blamed the London government. Churchill and Roosevelt furiously requested permission for Allied planes to land and refuel behind Soviet lines after dropping supplies to the Homeland Army. Stalin refused. Some consider this refusal the beginning of the cold war. On August 9, our squadron heard about the Warsaw uprising for the first time.

The only direct help the Homeland Army received during the Warsaw uprising was an amphibious assault across the Vistula from the infantry battalion of the Polish Berling Army. Since there was no adequate Soviet artillery support, and we were not authorized to provide air support, the battalion retreated with great losses. Our Commander-in-Chief, General Berling, was dismissed shortly thereafter. Many thought his dismissal was for authorizing this action to help the insurgents.

The Homeland Army finally surrendered to the Germans on October 2, 1944. On Hitler's orders, Warsaw was razed to the ground. Some *250,000* of its inhabitants, the vast majority of them civilians, died -- massacred by German and Ukrainian units during the uprising or buried in cellars where they had taken refuge.

Our squadron's first combat missions did not take place until the end of August. They consisted of sorties, some 150 miles south of Warsaw in support of the Soviet bridgehead on the west bank of the

Vistula. Luftwaffe opposition was light. Still, we counted with foreboding the number of our returning planes. Rumor had it that our first combat casualty was really a desertion: One of our Polish fighter pilots bailed out over enemy territory and surrendered to the Germans for no good reason other than his disgust over Stalin's betrayal. Another pilot was shot down over friendly territory and reappeared no worse for the experience. Our score was one confirmed Luftwaffe aircraft downed and another likely.

The Soviets did not "liberate" what was left of Warsaw until January 17, 1945. Stalin won his game and the fate of Poland was sealed.

Pilot and Rear Gunner of *IL-2*
(canopy open)

Chapter 18

Hitler Kaput

Ever since my miraculous rescue in Odessa, I had an inner feeling that I was obligated -- even driven -- to do something significant for the war effort. Just being part of the ground crew was a big letdown for me. But I finally got a chance to transcend my radio mechanic experience into a more meaningful flying experience.

In September, 1944, I had been given orders to attend a short rear gunner training session that included flying procedures, aircraft recognition instructions, and gunnery target practice. A group of us underwent this training because Soviet field experience showed that rear gunners were shot up more often than pilots in air combat, so a reserve was needed. I was ready and willing to fly.

One day in the radio shop, a Shturmovik wing commander told us that he needed to improve communication with the ground observer. I volunteered to install another radio in the gunner position so I could monitor the ground observer frequency while the wing commander directed his wing. He agreed to try it. I quickly arranged for a spare radio from the shop and installed it in the rear gunner position of his plane.

I remember my first flight on the IL-2, the roar of the engines and the slow lazy takeoff. My stomach was somewhere near my throat as the pilot did low-altitude dives. Many years later when I learned how to fly, I wondered how I ever flew sitting backwards, with absolutely no control over my destiny.

In my first sortie, we flew to a bend in the Vistula, a bridgehead on the western bank of the river held by Soviet and Polish forces. They were trying to expand the bridgehead against fierce German opposition. As we approached, I communicated with the ground observer. When we were a few miles from the target, I linked the wing commander to the ground observer. The commander then received and confirmed a description of the target: a fortified machine gun nest. At the wing commander's order, I disconnected him from the communication link so he could concentrate on directing the attack of the wing's three airplanes on the target while I maintained contact with the ground observer. After our pass over the target, our troops attempted to move closer to the machine gun nests with no success. We circled around and repeated the attack. Three passes were needed before the machine gun nests were actually silenced.

I was thrilled to be finally flying, but from my backward-facing rear gunner position, I could not see the ground or the attack, or the shells headed our way for that matter -- a decidedly unpleasant feeling. But I could hear our cannon fire and I could certainly feel the pullout from a dive and see the exploding flack and tracer bullets that missed us.

I later flew a half dozen more ground-support sorties and the wing commander liked the results. He asked the squadron commander if he could make the arrangement into a permanent assignment. I had done my job well, but there was a problem with this assignment if there was a German fighter attack. The squadron commander came to the same conclusion: The extra jury-rigged radio could interfere with the ease of operation of the gunner's gun. "No go," said the squadron commander, and this was the end of my World War II flying career. I went back to the ground crew for the duration.

First Fighter Regiment Warszawa
Photo of a remarkably true-to-life model[9]

In the autumn, our obsolescent Yak-1 fighters were exchanged for new Yak-9s and the First Polish Army was assigned to the Second Belarussian Front commanded by Marshal Konstantin Rokossovski. My unit, the First Fighter Squadron, became the First Fighter Regiment Warszawa, a part of the newly organized First Polish Composite Air Division, with IL-2s forming the Third Ground Attack Squadron of the Division. The Division also included the Second Night-Bomber Squadron. These bombers were a strange anachronism, since one would expect to see PO-2 biplanes as crop dusters or maybe in film footage of dogfights during World War I. They would pick up altitude, glide silently but slowly over the target at night and drop small bombs. Their stealth saved them from being shot down by ground fire -- sometimes.

The Germans also updated their fighter planes: I saw a German Messerschmidt 262, the first operational jet fighter in the world. It flew over our airfield and made a very distinct sound. The speed of the airplane was staggering. I was glad that I saw it from the ground and not the air. We had nothing to match it. Fortunately, the Luftwaffe only had a few of them on the Eastern front.

After the October fall of the Homeland Army in Warsaw, our airfield opened up for landing and refueling of British and American bombers and fighter escorts, after they flew over Germany. This gave me my first opportunity to send letters with the American aircrews to my Aunt Nettie in Philadelphia. My aunt told me after the war that she could never figure out what was going on and where I actually was. She would receive one letter from Italy, and the next from Africa, and a third would be postmarked from England, all within a short time.

The landing of an American Super Fortress was always an event that drew a large crowd on the Lublin airfield. During one of those autumn gatherings, Siunek Littman, a sharp-eyed contemporary of mine from my hometown of Drohobycz, recognized me. He served with an anti-aircraft battery assigned to defend the airfield. This was my first and very moving contact with my past. From him I received some news of Drohobycz, now liberated from the Germans. I wrote to Drohobycz, but received no news of my father or my sister. The scope of the disaster to the Jewish community there was becoming evident.

While writing this memoir, an emotional reunion with Siunek took place in June of 1999, 55 years after the Lublin meeting. Siunek, who Americanized his name to George Oscar Lee is now retired and lives in Florida. He has published two books based on World War II themes.

One day our Lublin airfield was "bombed" by a high-flying German reconnaissance plane. The German pilot saw the airfield, but had no bombs and so, as a practical joke, he jettisoned his wing-mounted empty auxiliary fuel tanks with excellent aim. The empty tanks made an awful whizzing sound coming down, probably noisier than the 1,000-pound bomb I was expecting as I heard it drop right outside the plane where I did my work. I hit the ground hard, covered my head with my hands, and watched my life pass through my eyes. In seconds, I heard the thud of impact and waited for it to explode -- and waited for another five very long minutes. Nothing happened. I was relieved when someone yelled empty fuel tanks had been dropped, not bombs.

On January 14, 1945, Marshal Rokossovski's offensive began in the midst of a heavy snowstorm. Apparently, Stalin rushed the offensive forward on Churchill's request to relieve the Battle of the Bulge that raged in the West. When the weather improved, we started flying non-stop sorties against the Germans around the Magnuszew Vistula bridgehead, south of Warsaw, where I saw my earlier air combat. The Soviet superiority was 11 to 1 in infantry, 7 to 1 in tanks, and 20 to 1 in artillery.[10] On a typical day, the Soviets flew 3,400 sorties compared with 40 German sorties. Not surprisingly, the Soviet offensive was an immediate and fast success and is considered one of the grandest strategic operations of the war.

On January 17, our First Polish Berling Army occupied Warsaw. Eyewitnesses told us how they stepped in horrified silence through the desert of frozen rubble. Behind them, wrapped against the savage frost, followed a group of men, the new Polish Communist

Government headed by Edward Osobka-Morawski and Boleslaw Bierut.

Krakow was liberated on January 19. By the end of January, the Soviets were on the German river Oder, only 50 miles east of Berlin, having traversed the 300 miles west from the Vistula River where the offensive had begun. Most Polish territory was now freed of Germans. With this rapid advance as the offensive unfolded, the Lublin airfield was too far from the front. In February, the ground crews were flown on DC-3s to our new airfield in the vicinity of Bydgoszcz, about halfway between Warsaw and Berlin. I continued working as a ground crew radio mechanic.

On April 16, just a few days after my twentieth birthday, the final offensive against Berlin began. In spite of their hopeless situation, the Germans put up a stubborn defense of their capital. Soviet forces, including the First Polish Army deployed north of Berlin, had to fight hard for every yard with staggering losses on both sides. For the first time in the war, our Squadron was involved in aerial battles. Over fifty engagements resulted in nine German fighters being shot down and two of our planes lost. Fortunately, both of our pilots parachuted to safety.

By the end of April, the ring around Berlin tightened. Our airfield was moved again to a town called Rathenow, about forty miles west of Berlin. Only 20 more miles to the west beyond Berlin was the river Elbe, the demarcation line that eventually separated us from the U.S. Ninth Army.

On April 20th, Hitler's birthday, we could see a huge flotilla of American bombers flying their last mission to bomb Berlin.

On April 30th, Hitler committed suicide, and the seat of Hitler's government, the Reichstag, and Hitler's chancellery fell.

On May 2, Berlin surrendered.

On the evening of May 7, 1945, news spread that Admiral Karl Doenitz, Hitler's successor, signed the surrender document. A crewman came running into our quarters and shouted: "The war is over! Germany surrendered!" At this time, six of us were quartered in a private German home. We hugged and danced with joy.

It seemed strange the next day, May 8, the official VE day was so ordinary. The sun didn't shine any brighter. There were no fireworks and no parades. In fact, our squadron still flew a few reconnaissance missions just to make sure all of the Germans had gotten the message. I said a quiet inner prayer of thanks. I had survived the war. I had outlived Hitler! Sara's blessing had indeed protected me.

Part 4

Iron Curtain

Chapter 19

Fallen Berlin

On May 8, 1945, the Squadron received a victory bonus. We were allowed to see Berlin. The day after Germany surrendered, I saw the Reichstag, the seat of the Nazi government, now flying the red Soviet flag. This seemed to be proof positive Germany was defeated. Not much more than the walls of the Reich's chancellery still stood. It was surreal. We knew that this had been Hitler's last hangout, but on this day it was still hard to believe the rumors of Hitler's death were true.

I could not see a single undamaged building, yet curiously, the sign for the U-Bahn subway still hung over the stairs that now only led to black, water-flooded nothingness. The remains of houses still standing among bomb craters were just empty silent walls, windowless and roofless. Enormous pyramids of red and yellow rubble lent macabre relief to the monotony of the scene. A few main streets had been cleared; most side streets were impassable. There was a pervasive stench of rotting flesh, the smell of death. The bodies of many German soldiers still had not been cleared. Some of them were ground into the dirt by tanks, some twisted with the military hardware they were operating when the end came. Here and there, I could see a severed limb so soaked in blood that the nationality of the uniform was hard to determine.

There were few German civilians walking the streets. All had the look of suffering, shock, and emptiness seared across their faces. I passed by the main railroad station with the handsome Victorian facade grotesquely preserved next to the indistinguishable mounds of rubble that represented the rest of the building. The tracks were twisted and scorched and led to nowhere. The same place the war led all of us.

At the end of the day, we rode back to the airfield in an open truck. The road was crowded with civilian refugees. I happened to see two unarmed men in uniform, one of them limping very badly. At first, I did not recognize the uniforms. Then, I realized they were Americans. I banged on the roof of the driver's cab and after some argument, I convinced him to stop and give the Americans a ride.

I put my meager knowledge of English to use for the first time and greeted the soldiers. I never had English in school. But while in the ghetto in Drohobycz, my grandmother had given me a beginner's English textbook that had belonged to my aunt Regina. Learning English was wonderful for my morale. The very idea that she thought I would ever use it implied that she thought I would survive the war.

Our new passengers, Frank Ambrose and Hans Schwartzkopf, were American prisoners of war, liberated from a German camp by the Red Army. They were captured in the Italian campaign in 1943. They were both privates. Frank was from Pennsylvania and Hans from New York City. Rather than wait for official arrangements to repatriate them, they decided to head for the American lines on their own. This proved harder than they anticipated. They were tired and hungry, and Ambrose had sprained his ankle and was in pain. We took them to our Squadron. There I found them a room on a farm where we were quartered, and I persuaded the cook to feed them for a couple of days until I managed to get them a ride to the river Elbe. All they had to do once they were there was to cross the river to reach the U.S. Army. Frank was particularly grateful since he was in no shape to walk. As a parting gesture, he gave me his dog tag. "If you ever need help from American GIs, show them this dog tag and tell them that you helped us in need," he said. I stuck it under the cover of Sara's diary and thought of it as a nice souvenir. Little did I know how important the dog tag would become.

The next day, it was the other radio technicians' turn for leave. My friend Nicolay headed for nearby town. He and a mechanic from the squadron saw a bottle of Cognac by the roadside. It was booby-trapped by the Germans. The mechanic picked up the bottle and was killed instantly; Nicolay was seriously injured. They were the last war casualties in our squadron. The war had ended, but not the mayhem.

I visited Nicolay in the army field hospital in Rathenow, a few days after his accident. The hospital was housed in big tents. Someone directed me to Nicolay's bed. It was just as well, because I wouldn't have recognized him. His head was bandaged and his face contorted with pain. What do you say to someone who had had the bad luck to get blasted by a booby trap, three days after the war has ended?

"Nicolay, your doctor says you will be fine," was the best that I could come up with. "I feel so stupid," whispered Nicolay, with some effort. "All of this over a bottle of booze. Never thought drinking was that bad for your health." He tried to smile but grimaced instead. I changed the subject by filling him in on news of the Squadron. When a man next to Nicolay started screaming in pain and blood trickled from his mouth, a nurse ran in to help him and told me to clear out. I was grateful for an excuse to go.

I walked the mile back to my quarters along a rural road. The smell of rotting flesh still permeated the warm spring air. By now, most of the human corpses were cleared from the roads, but very bloated bodies of dead cows were scattered in the fields and contributed to the aroma of death. I wondered where I was going, even though I knew exactly where this road was taking me. It was beginning to sink in that, with the war over, my perspective had changed. I was 20 years old and I wondered where my grandmother's grandson was headed. Was her prophecy that I would end up living in America going to materialize?

Halfway back to camp, I heard screams coming from behind a barn. Six Soviet soldiers, armed with submachine guns, were clustered together. The screams came from a young German boy, maybe thirteen, who was pounding his fists on one of the soldiers. I ran closer; close enough to see the drunken full-moon Mongol faces of the soldiers, descendants of the Golden Horde of Genghis Khan. For centuries, they ruled Russia and were a scourge to their neighbors. Now, they were back in Europe in our front sector, in Soviet uniforms.

A woman was being held on the ground by two of the soldiers while another raped her to the rhythmic clapping of the surrounding comrades. "*Muti, Muti*" (Mommy, Mommy in German), the boy yelled in a futile attempt to rescue his mother. One of the soldiers reached for him, but the boy grabbed a rake with a long handle and swung it at the soldier. *Yob tvoyu mat*, yelled the soldier in pain. How ironic, I thought. The curse translates as, "Fuck your mother," and that was exactly what they were doing. The boy started to take another swing at the soldier, but did not finish. A volley of bullets from an automatic hit him. He recoiled from the impact and a fountain of blood squirted from his chest.

At this point, the drunken Mongol noticed me. He pointed his gun at me and yelled, "Get lost soldier, or you will get the same." He was drunk enough to do it. I ran back to my unit and reported the incident. "Can we do something to save the woman?" I asked the duty officer. "They will kill her, too!" He shrugged his shoulders. "Are you crazy, Sergeant? Just look around at what is going on. Forget it and go back to your unit." I went back to my unit, but I never forgot.

In the first few weeks of the Soviet occupation of Germany, rape and plunder of the German population were not isolated incidents but a mass frenzy. Much has been said about the troops' desire to get even for German atrocities by committing atrocities of their own, while the authorities looked the other way. To me, it didn't look like revenge was the motive.

I made sergeant by the end of the war

There were millions of young men deprived of sexual release for a long time. This was a chance for some to realize whatever desires they felt, and sex was high on the list. Soldiers were armed and civilians were at their mercy. Some soldiers took advantage of this.

German women soon realized that reluctance led to violence. By natural evolution, the most common transaction was sexual favor in exchange for food and sometimes for more permanent protection from roving bands of soldiers.

Plunder was widespread. Many soldiers expropriated whatever was valuable and easy to carry. Wristwatches were high on the priority list for Russians, who valued them as a sign of wealth and importance. It was quite common to see Russian soldiers with three or four wristwatches proudly worn on both arms. In the final analysis, without fear of punishment, what a soldier did or did not do at that time depended mostly on his desires, values, and ethics.

After a while, the Soviet upper echelons realized that closing their eyes to atrocities was poisoning any future chances of cooperation with the Germans. It also gave the Soviet Army, in the eyes of the Western Allies, the reputation of being undisciplined barbarians. Firm measures were put into effect to "civilize" the troops, and after a few summary executions, major atrocities against civilians stopped in a few months.

Chapter 20

Between a Rock and a Hard Place

In July, 1945, the Soviet command ordered the withdrawal of all Polish units to Poland. Our Squadron Warszawa moved near Modlin, an old strategic fort 25 miles northwest of Warsaw where the two longest Polish rivers, the Vistula and the Bug, meet. I remember the river junction well. As part of our peacetime training, after the 6 a.m. wake-up bugle call, we had to run a mile to the river junction and go for a compulsory swim. The water was treacherous, because the mixing of the rivers caused whirlpools. "No problem," assured the first lieutenant in charge of physical training. "Just let the whirlpool suck you to the bottom and then swim away." I wondered what I would do for oxygen on the way down. My concerns were not groundless. One morning after our swim, we noticed a clump of unclaimed clothes when we dressed. We had lost a comrade. No one even noticed his drowning; his body was never found. Our swimming routine was then moved a few hundred yards down the Vistula.

Daily after breakfast, we marched to the airfield for endless, and now to me pointless, flight training. Every other evening, we received a mentally suffocating political propaganda lecture on the greatness of Stalin and his Polish surrogates. Every few weeks I had a day off, with precious few places to go. Warsaw was nearby, but most of it was still in ruins. There was no promise of demobilization, just the opposite, in fact. We were now "valued veterans" and would form the cadres of the new "democratic" Polish Air Force. Rumors were even circulated that many of us, including me, were going to be sent to Officer's Training School.

Without the rationale of fighting the Germans, my situation in Poland became unbearable. On one hand, there was the over-bearing communist government, using oppression and brutality to suppress the Polish national desire for freedom. On the other hand, there was the virulent unofficial anti-Semitism of many Poles, which did not diminish after the slaying of millions of their Jewish neighbors by the Nazis. Instead, anti-Semitism was reawakened by a new excuse: A few thousand of some 100,000 Polish Jews returning from the Soviet Union occupied the high echelons of the Polish Communist party and the secret police, often attempting to fully assimilate and disguise their Jewish background. The Stalinists, who understood the value of Jews as historical scapegoats, recruited them in a shrewd move. For most returning Jews, the prospects of life in the Soviet Union were simply so dismal that just about all returned to Poland after the war.

Many Poles, to this day, blame the brutal Stalinist post-war occupation on the Polish Jews. It was certainly a widely held view while I was there. An example is the statement by Primate August J. Hlond who at the time headed the Catholic Church in Poland, in connection with a bloody Polish post-war pogrom in Kielce in 1946. While condemning the murder of Jews, he felt they brought it on themselves: "The fact that conditions are worsening should in large part be attributed to the Jews today, occupying leading positions in the Polish government and attempting to introduce a governmental structure which the majority of the nation does not desire."[11]

Primate Hlond's myopic and anti-Semitic view ignored the fact that a vast majority of Polish Jews opted to return to Poland because they were disillusioned with communism, and many of them suffered Soviet prisons and gulags. Yet, Jews were often stereotyped by the Polish Catholic Church as communists and traitors, polarizing the situation and making departure to the West the only choice for a non-communist Jew. This caused a self-fulfilling prophecy —

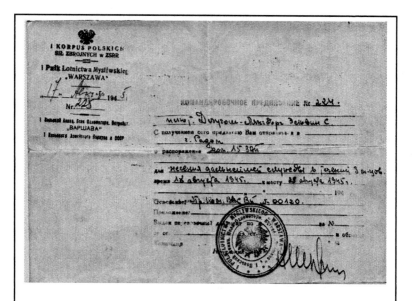

Officer's Training School Orders

1st Corps of Polish
Armed Forces
1st Fighter squadron
"WARSZAWA"
17 August 1945
No. 225

(translation from Russian)

Travel Order No. 224

Sergeant Dlugosh-Langberg Edwin S.
Upon receipt of this, you are ordered to travel to the
town of Radom to continue there for further service
for 3 months Depart 18 August 1945 and report on
28 August 1945
Reason: Air Force Order No. 00120
Commanding Officer: Col. Miklaszewicz

eventually, the majority of Jews remaining in Poland were indeed communists.

Most Poles ignored the reality that in every Soviet-occupied country, with or without Jews, the same brutal communist government structure was put in place. Poland's independence was lost on the day Soviet troops marched in. Short of starting World War III, no one could have done anything about the sovietization of Poland. If the Jews were not handy, the Soviets would have had no difficulty in promoting a few more ethnic Polish communists to higher positions.

Since the Jews in power could not be "got at," hatred was vented on the innocents. According to official statistics, 150 Jews died in hate murders at the hands of Poles in the first quarter of 1945. From April to August, 81 more Jews were killed and 13 injured in 30 attacks. On August 11, a Polish mob attacked a synagogue and adjacent Jewish homes in Krakow. Every episode of anti-Semitic violence played right into Stalin's hands, because it reduced sympathy and resolve in the West to oppose the loss of Polish independence to the Soviets.

I despised the communists in power for selling their souls to the lie of "a workers' paradise" and closing their eyes to the daily evidence of brutality and oppression. Even more, I despised the ease with which the ingrained Polish anti-Semitism could be manipulated, so that even after the Nazi Holocaust more Jews were killed just for being Jews. Escape from Poland seemed like the only way out for me.

My response to the rumors of an upcoming transfer to Officer's Training School was to start a campaign of misbehavior in hopes my commanders would reconsider my promotion and get rid of me. The infractions were minor, but frequent and persistent. I was late for roll call, late from leave, late for everything, and I pretended not to hear commands. I received unheeded warnings until I was locked up for a day in our unit's brig.

Ironically, I was released from the brig a few hours early because my dreaded orders were received. Going to Officer's Training School

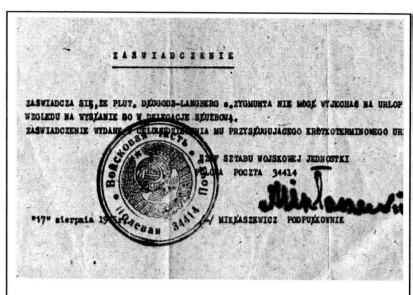

Certificate of Leave

To get a little more time for my plans, I pleaded for a leave. It was granted for the ten days between my departure from Modlin and for my ordered arrival date in Radom for Officer's Training School.

Translation (from Polish}

<u>CERTIFICATION</u>

It is certified that Sergeant Dlugosh–Langberg, son of Zygmunt could not take his leave because he was sent on service assignment. This certificate is issued for the purpose of granting him a short leave.

Chief of Staff of Military Unit
Field Post Office 34414

17 August 1945   Col. Miklaszewicz

in Radom, some 60 miles south of Warsaw, would condemn me to a professional military career. I was clearly at a crossroads in my life: a dismal future in the Polish military or desertion. The punishment for desertion was clear. Even though World War II was over, there was no peace in Poland. Armia Krajowa and their splinter paramilitary groups were not quite finished off by the Soviets. A deserter, if caught, would be shot. There were also friendships with my comrades to consider, and memories of a long war service.

It was August 18, 1945. My orders were processed quickly. I pleaded for a "family leave" since I had not had one since my service started, and I received a ten-day leave before I had to report to Radom. I briefly thought of the possibility of going to Drohobycz but gave up this idea, because it involved crossing the border between Poland and the USSR, and I had no taste for that. I said my goodbyes and, by the next morning, I was in a small local two-track railroad station. It was a clear and hot August day and I was sweating profusely, not so much from the heat as from inner turmoil. I debated my two alternatives back and forth: a career in the Soviet-controlled Polish military or desertion. It was not an easy decision.

Finally, I decided to let fate make the choice. If the first train that arrived was going south in the direction of the Officers School in Radom, I would go there. If the train went in the opposite direction, I would go toward the western borders of Poland and desert. The outcome could not be predicted. At the time, there were no such things as railroad schedules. One would just go to the station and stay there until the right train came along. The first train that pulled into the station was going northwest toward Torun. The train had a couple of passenger cars that were filled to the brim and half-dozen boxcars. I jumped into a boxcar through the wide open door. There was no looking back. In ten days, Sergeant Dlugosh Langberg would be a deserter.

Chapter 21

Out of Poland

My desertion was unplanned and spur-of-the moment; yet, it was a difficult decision. But once I was on a westbound train, I felt an inner peace that I hadn't known for a long while. I knew I had made the right decision. I would not be condemned to living a lie by forever straddling my Polish and Jewish identities. Other than going towards the border, I had no clear plan of action -- but at least my military travel papers were valid for ten days.

At the time, the post-war expansion of Soviet borders to the west included a Stalinist twist. The shift of borders was combined with ethnic cleansing on a scale that has probably never been duplicated in history. Millions of people were on the move. The ethnic Polish population from the prewar eastern territories, now annexed by the Soviets, was shoved into Poland. Ethnic Germans were pushed out of the newly acquired Polish territory that was carved out of Germany. Soviet policy made sure the old boundaries were permanently obliterated, and so they remain to the present day.

Polish workers who were shipped into Germany during the war were returning to Poland. The few Jewish survivors of the Holocaust in Poland, and other Polish Jews returning from the Soviet Union, were leaving Poland in droves. They traveled through

Czechoslovakia to "displaced persons" camps in the U.S.-occupied zone of Germany. From there, they eventually went to Israel or the United States. What was a difficult and individual decision for me, arrived at without any group contact or pressure, was in retrospect just the motion of a molecule in a torrent.

Few of the participants of this massive population movement had any form of identification. Looking around at the chaos on the train, and considering my years of experience in escaping through the immeasurably better organized war time German and Soviet police controls, I felt escape from Poland should not be much of a challenge. Since I did not acquire any loot in Germany and my military pay was a pittance, I had very little money. This was my main problem. I consoled myself as I sat on top of my pack on the floor of the train: Tomorrow is another day and I will think of something. I ate my ration and dozed off.

A commotion interfered with my sleep. "Hey, Yid, what are you carrying? Give it to us!" That woke me up. I could hardly believe my ears. Hadn't the Nazis been defeated? I jumped up and rushed into the fray. Three burly Poles in their early twenties were hustling two Jewish couples. One of the Poles was trying to wrench a suitcase from a slight Jewish man in his forties. I boiled with fury. The memory of the blackmail of the young Jewish man for gold coins in front of the Lvov railroad station flashed in front of my eyes.

This time, I knew I could do something about it. I grabbed the hollering Pole by his lapel with one hand, and hit him as hard as I could in the stomach with the other. I must have been in pretty good shape, because the man, at least an inch taller than me, doubled up, gasping for breath. The pilfered suitcase fell to the floor. I faced his two companions. They thought of pouncing on me, but then decided that attacking a uniformed soldier was too much of a risk. They grabbed their moaning companion, cursed at me and disappeared at the next station.

Leopold, the man whose suitcase I saved, thanked me profusely and asked me to join them. Leopold introduced me to his sister Lisa and another couple traveling with them. Before the war, they all lived in a town not too far from my own. They left with the retreating Russians and spent the war in Russia. They had come back to Poland some months earlier and made their livelihood as peddlers. They could not very well be called black marketers, because there was not much of an organized "white" market at the time in Poland. The local price differentials in the eastern and western provinces were quite high, so their operation was profitable. They looked Jewish, spoke heavily accented Polish, and traveled with a mountain of luggage that exposed them to sporadic attacks, like the one I had just witnessed.

As we got to know each other better, Leopold made me a proposition: "Why don't you become our bodyguard and also help us carry our merchandise (about a half ton of it) for which we will give you a generous cut of our profits?" I agreed, provided it was a short-term deal -- three days to be exact -- and at the end, they would provide, in addition to some money, a set of civilian clothes that fit. I explained why I needed it. We shook hands on the deal.

We had a nice meal together on the train and Lisa showed me my "bedroom." It was an opening she fashioned from a pile of her bags and suitcases in a corner of the boxcar with a comfortable blanket on the bottom. In a little while, she joined me. She was plain and twice my age, but her body felt well preserved. It had been a good while for me and I was grateful. Afterwards I fell asleep in her arms, thinking the life of a deserter was not as bad as it was cracked up to be.

We traveled and got on and off the train with the cases. The group traded in Torun and Katowice. Not a single MP asked for my papers. There were no more attacks to repel, but carting the merchandise was hard work. On the third day, we arrived in Krakow, where we parted company. Lisa was not heartbroken about our parting. She warmly greeted her husband, who waited for her at the railroad station. I changed into the civilian outfit they provided. I also had a suitcase with a change of clothing and more money than I would have earned in a year in the Air Force. It was not a fortune, but just enough Polish zlotys to keep me going for a few weeks.

Leopold had given me the address of the Jewish refugee and community center in Krakow. It was a small office with huge bulletin boards, covered with notes organized by the originator's pre-war town of residence. The notes asked for news and in turn, provided news and addresses. I looked for Drohobycz and much to my delight, I found a half-dozen notices. One attracted my immediate attention. It was a note from Dr. Bruno Kupferberg, a lawyer and a colleague of my Uncle Elias. He had returned from the Soviet Union and now lived in Krakow with his family. I decided to pay him a visit.

I was touched by the warm reception of the Kupferbergs. They were delighted to see another survivor from their hometown and they insisted I stay with them. Before I accepted, I told them that I was a deserter and this would expose them to some risk. Dr. Kupferberg clearly understood and approved of my motives. The risk did not faze him at all. After a Polish attack on a synagogue in his neighborhood a few weeks earlier, he, too, realized that after the Holocaust, Poland would never again be a place for Jews. He knew it was only a matter of time until he would have to get out of Poland also. He was determined to help me in my escape.

The next day, Dr. Kupferberg took me to a photographer. When the picture was ready, he took me to his dingy office where he introduced me to his law partner, Henryk Chajes. As it turns out, Henryk was a distant cousin on my grandmother Lauterbach's side of the family. The two lawyers prepared a very legal-looking notarized affidavit certifying my true identity. The affidavit embellished the truth a bit by saying I had just returned from forced labor in Germany. The affidavit was issued on the 28th day of August, 1945, the very day I was supposed to report at Radom for my officer training. Instead it was my self-administered "demobilization" date.

At the time, Jews escaping from Poland only had rudimentary help and struggled on their own. Later the "underground railway" was much better organized and transported thousands of Jews at a time. Still, I later received some good guidance from the Jewish

This is the affidavit, generously prepared for me by Dr. Kupferberg and Henryk Chajes. The photo shows the set of clothes that I earned on my train ride as the bodyguard.

center. The escape route led through Cieszyn, a border town with Czechoslovakia, some 80 miles southwest of Krakow. Through the Kupferbergs, I managed to exchange some of my Polish zloty for Czech crowns. I joined forces with two other fellows about my age, whom I met at the Jewish Center and who just happened to be ready to take the trip. They had recently returned from the USSR and were headed for Palestine.

One day early in September, I said my goodbyes to the Kupferbergs and joined my two companions to take the train from Krakow to Bielsko. There we boarded a shuttle train to the border at Cieszyn. The bulk of the passengers were Jews trying to get out of Poland and the Pol-ish border police did not attempt to interfere. They only looked for and detained Polish escapees, presumably political opponents of the Communist regime. To me, an expert at crossing borders, it was amazing these Poles got themselves detained. All they had to do was say they were Jewish to get waved goodbye out of Poland.

Things were not as easy on the Czech side. We knew from passengers on the train who had previously tried to cross the border that a Czech visa was required. If you did not have a Czech visa, the border guards would immediately return you to the Polish shuttle train. By a Polish-Czech agreement, the shuttle train waited an extra half hour for rejected passengers before departing back to Bielsko. Not one of the three of us had either a visa or enough money to offer the border guards a bribe. But I had a plan.

We would jump from the train a bit early and skirt the border gate. Later, we would sneak into the Czech part of Cieszyn (spelled Tesin there). We would then avoid the railroad station until a few minutes before the 9 p.m. departure of the train for Bran and Prague. In Czechoslovakia the trains did run on schedule! Only local passengers would be boarding the train then, since there was no shuttle train at that hour. Compared with my war experiences, this was almost a game. Of course, I was an experienced "train jumper".

If the others did not break a leg, the worst consequence they could suffer was to be returned back to Poland.

We managed to sneak into the street in back of the Czech railroad station. It was only late afternoon, but -- as with my plan that worked so well in Odessa -- we looked for a lady of the evening who could provide a safe place to hide. We walked into a suitably disrespectable dive and found a rather worn-out prostitute. We negotiated a price for the three of us, and she took us to her place. Plans, no matter how good, never quite work out the same way twice. When we explained to her she could keep the money, that we only wanted to hang around her place until dark, she balked. If we wanted to hang around, she insisted, at least one of us would have to perform, as agreed. We drew straws and, much to my relief, I did not win.

At a quarter to nine, we dashed for the railroad station, got our tickets, and, just as the whistle blew, hopped on the train for Prague. Once on Czech territory and away from the border, we were no longer subject to forcible return to Poland. We were now officially "Displaced Persons."

Chapter 22

Zigzag through the Curtain

We arrived in Prague at the crack of dawn. My traveling companions knew some people in town and we parted company. The city was still very quiet. I was amazed that the streets, buildings, and bridges were seemingly untouched by the war. All signs of the German occupation were gone. Prague was the most beautiful city I had ever seen. Years later, I saw Paris and as far as I am concerned, it didn't even come close to the beauty of Prague. Of course, I looked at Prague with the eyes of a 20 year old and at Paris with the eyes of a seasoned 40 year old.

The people in Krakow had given me the address of a refugee camp in Prague run by the United Nations Relief and Rehabilitation Administration. Since Czech and Polish are similar Slavic languages, I did not have a hard time getting directions. I hopped on a trolley and rode through Prague to the camp.

When I reached the camp, much to my surprise, I discovered it was a temporarily converted movie house. The marquee was still there with the faded title of the last movie shown. I was processed into the camp in a friendly and simple way. I only had to give them my name and where I was headed. They gave me the number of my bunk and some food. The vast floor was covered with hundreds of bunks, separated into three slices. Males were next to the screen. Families were in the middle, and females were at the far end. Except for impossibly overcrowded bathroom facilities, the place was not bad. I stayed there for free, but had to contribute several hours a day to help with maintenance. It was a five-star accommodation compared to some of the camps I stayed in during the war.

I was told that transports to the U.S. zone of Germany left about once a week, but in the last couple of weeks, transports had stopped. The U.S. zone of occupation was my objective because it was the closest gateway to the West and away from the Soviet sphere of influence. I would have to stay in the camp in Prague and wait. I spent my free time wandering about Prague, visiting museums, and playing tourist -- as long as the attractions were free.

Czechoslovakia in the first years after the war ended was a unique country. It managed for a while to be friendly with both the Soviets and the West. You could be an outspoken Communist or an anticommunist and it made no difference. Both political movements participated in the government. Czechs have a long tradition of bending and flexing with the shifting winds of history. The Czechoslovak government in exile during World War II, headed by President Edvard Benesh in London, realized early in the game that the Soviets would emerge as a dominant power in central Europe. Unlike the London Poles, Benesh did not object when the Soviets demanded that Czechoslovakia cede its eastern territories to the Soviet Union.

Prague had been liberated from German occupation by Soviet troops. At least, this is what is generally believed. In fact, Prague was actually freed by the Vlasov Army, composed of Russian prisoners of war who chose to fight on the side of Germany rather than die of starvation in German POW camps. The Vlasov Army found itself near Prague at the end of the war and, in an attempt to endear itself to the allies, switched sides and decided to aid the insurrection in Prague against the Germans. This was extremely lucky for Prague, because it prevented the destruction of the city.

At the time, General George Patton and his U.S. Army troops were only 60 miles from Prague, with no German opposition. Soviet agents had quickly infiltrated the leadership of the uprising in Prague and the Soviets requested that Patton not occupy the city. Patton, whether by his own initiative or on instructions from Washington, obliged and remained in Pilsen, a southwestern Czech town known for its excellent beer. The Soviet occupation of Prague signified to Stalin that this was his turf, priming Czechoslovakia for an eventual communist takeover. The Vlasov Army had no chance to surrender to the Americans, and the surrender to the Soviets had consequences.

As I enjoyed myself in Prague, I came across a sobering reminder of who was really the boss. I wandered by a building housing the headquarters of the Czech communist party. A huge picture of Stalin glared at me, as if saying, "Langberg, you can run, but you can't hide from me. I will get you yet!" The years of communist brainwashing had not been totally wasted on me. I didn't end up admiring Stalin, but I was surely scared of him. On the spot, I made a decision: no more hanging around Prague, waiting for the convoy. I had to get across the American line at Pilsen without delay." I returned to the movie house camp, collected my belongings and hopped on the train for Pilsen.

The train got to the America zone in a few hours and then U.S. Army MPs entered the train. Czech citizens were allowed to pass, but my Kupferberg identification document wasn't good enough. The MPs took me off the train, along with a group of other people with flaky papers.

I assessed my situation and decided an attempt at escape into the U.S. zone at this point was futile. Three MPs guarded our group. The American side of the demarcation line consisted of a fence of razor wire patrolled by MPs. With grudging admiration, I had to admit the officer in charge of security knew his job. My border-crossing talents could not match his. His was a military talent ironically wasted on preventing refugees from reaching freedom from the Reds. I pleaded in broken English with the MPs to let me go. A U.S. officer in charge advised me to go to the Office of the Military Attaché in Prague, since only that office could authorize passes for non-Czechs. We were all escorted back to the train and back to Prague we went. That was that. I was back in the movie house again.

The fear of Stalin persisted. The next morning, I decided to go to the Office of the Military Attaché at the American Embassy. The embassy was located in a beautiful medieval part of town, facing the presidential palace called Hradcany. The sergeant on duty was not too eager to listen to me until I showed him the dog tag from Frank Ambrose, the American ex-POW I had helped the previous May near Berlin. The sergeant took the dog tag and came back in a while with his superior, a somewhat pudgy lieutenant in his early thirties. "I am Lieutenant Weisgall, Assistant Military Attaché," he introduced himself. "What is the story with this dog tag?" For a moment, I feared that the story of the tag was too naïve and would never work, but I spit it out anyway. "Frank told me that if I ever needed help from an American GI, I should produce the dog tag and tell him I helped a GI in need." Lt. Weisgall eyed me for a while as if trying to decide if he should believe my story. "OK," he said. "What is it that you want?" "I need a pass to cross the U.S. demarcation line at Pilsen." "I will do you one better," said Lt. Weisgall. "I am going to drive to Pilsen this afternoon. Be here at 3 p.m. and I will take you with me."

I left the embassy somewhat dazed. Should I believe the lieutenant? It bothered me that I still did not have a piece of paper entitling me to cross the checkpoint. What was the lieutenant going to do at the checkpoint? Needless to say, I was at the embassy well before three o'clock. The lieutenant showed up on time with an older civilian, gave me a GI coat and hat to wear and instructions: "Keep your mouth shut at the checkpoint." The civilian turned out to be a State Department visitor. Their reason for traveling to Pilsen was to attend U.S. Army services to celebrate Rosh Hashanah – the Jewish New Year -- in 1945.

On the way to Pilsen, Lt. Weisgall asked for my story. I told him first a few key facts. When I saw that he was clearly interested, I ended up telling him more and more details. The entire 60-mile trip was eventually taken up by my tale. "Eddie, you must write it all up," demanded Lt. Weisgall. I was glad he seemed interested in my story, and I promised I would oblige some day. But it was time for the crossing. I took a deep breath. The Soviet guards merely saluted our open jeep as Lt. Weisgall flashed his military pass and waved us through. The American MPs did likewise. After all of my worrying, that was it. We were through the demarcation line. I should mention the jeep had the ensign of a one-star General flying from the antenna -- Lieutenant Weisgall's little joke.

We arrived shortly at their hotel in Pilsen. The lieutenant invited me to their room. "Eddie, in the unlikely event that you should end up in a synagogue this evening, take a shower now in our bathroom. You need it." This was my first exposure to the American preoccupation with perfectly natural body smells. Another first was the shower curtain. I kept it outside the tub and caused a minor flood, requiring intervention of the hotel staff. In spite of this mishap, Lt. Weisgall asked me to lunch the next day. He said he wanted to discuss a proposition with me. I accepted and made my departure. I danced, rather than walked, to the UNRRA refugee camp in Pilsen where I was to spend the night. Happily I rejoiced: "Screw you, Uncle Joe Stalin. I got away!!"

The next day at lunch, Lt. Weisgall came right to the point. "Eddie, as an American diplomat, I just got assigned a beautiful villa in Prague. You can be on my domestic staff, live in the villa, and help me run things. You are clearly a resourceful guy, and I need someone like you." I despairingly said, "Lt. Weisgall, how can I possibly cross back? I am a deserter, it would not be safe."

"Call me Hugo," he said as he put his hand on my shoulder. "Eddie, you are not a deserter," he gravely pronounced like a judge. "Desertion is an act of cowardice. Your act was one of conviction and courage. You are a defector." With my meager knowledge of English at the time, this was a new word. But it somehow eased my conscience, if not my fears.

I wondered aloud how much good it would do me if Uncle Joe ever caught up with me. Hugo laughed: "Do you really think that the Soviets are combing Europe for a missing Polish Air Force sergeant? Besides, Czechoslovakia is an independent country and both American and Soviet troops are going to leave quite soon." He was reassuring: "I should be able to keep you out of trouble in Prague. Believe me, living in a diplomatic villa in Prague beats a DP camp in the U.S. zone of Germany any day while you are waiting for your U.S. visa. What do you think, Eddie?"

"I don't like being called Eddie," I thought. In any case, I thought, it should be spelled E-D-Y. I also thought I liked being in the U.S. zone without pictures of Stalin hanging over my head. But what I told Hugo was that I needed some time to think about it. He told me to show up at the hotel the next morning if I was interested. They would be returning to Prague then.

This time I did not dance my way back to the camp. Should I or shouldn't I go back? Was Czechoslovakia truly independent? Was I being paranoid in thinking whatever Stalin touched never became independent again? I decided with little conviction that Assistant Military Attaché, Lt. Hugo Weisgall should know a lot more than I did and I should listen to him. He also might be helpful in expediting my U.S. visa, my long-term dream.

I showed up the next morning. I donned the GI coat and hat again. We hopped into the jeep again and drove to the checkpoint. We were saluted by the MPs again. We passed unchallenged by the Soviet guards again. My God, I was back in the Soviet sphere ...again!

Chapter 23

Sunrise in Prague

To get some idea of the gigantic, overnight change in my life, look at this picture of Hugo's superb villa with me out front in an American uniform, sitting in a jeep. After years of sleeping on straw, spread on the ground, or at best a cot, and sharing a latrine with a hundred others, I now had a room of my own, a comfortable bed with a real spring mattress, and a modern bathroom right next to my room. The middle window on the top floor was mine. It was not the best room in the villa, but it definitely had one with the best views of Prague. The housekeeper and the maid occupied the other two rooms on the top floor.

Lt. Hugo Weisgall, the Assistant Military Attaché at the U.S. embassy in Prague shared this villa with Lieutenant Colonel (T.K.) Taylor, Air Attaché. Their bedrooms were on the second floor. T.K. was bemedaled, tall, skinny, and dapper and he sang off key. Hugo was short, pudgy, and an accomplished musician.

The main entrance on the ground floor opened into a grand foyer with an adjoining living room and dining room. The kitchen and pantry were in the back of the villa. The janitor, his wife, and their infant child lived in the basement. In the back of the villa was a garden on the slope of a hill and on the top was a small and empty

Here I am, driving a Jeep in front of the villa

astronomical observatory. Before the war, a Jewish industrialist owned this villa. Neither the amateur astronomer nor his family survived.

My role in the household was "special assignments" that mostly included furnishing and equipping the villa. Hugo did not treat me as a servant, but rather as sort of a protégé. Still, I ate in the kitchen with the cook and the maid and this suited me fine. My compensation was pocket money, room and board at this fabulous diplomatic villa, and Hugo's old uniforms for clothing. Good food was a lot more valuable in those days than money.

To help with my assignments, Hugo provided me with an old, beat-up Jeep and a German Luger pistol. The latter was an elegant sidearm worn by German officers during the war. The only time I ever drew it was when I once heard a commotion in the basement in the middle of the night. I ran down the stairs, gun drawn, only to find out it was a noisy marital argument between the janitor and his wife. The argument was instantly resolved when the combatants saw my gun and both implored, "DON'T SHOOT!" Of course, I had no intention of shooting but I was glad to be able to quickly restore domestic tranquility at 2 a.m.

The jeep was another story. I needed it and I used it. Our villa was on top of a steep hill, quite a distance from shops and the center of town. It never occurred to Hugo that a 20-year-old ex-Polish Air Force sergeant would not know how to drive. Fortunately, there was not much traffic outside of the villa. After a lot of jerky, gear-grinding starts and stops, I taught myself how to drive. T.K., the lanky, decorated former bomber pilot, after seeing me drive, told me he could drive backwards better than I could drive forwards, which was undoubtedly true.

Still, I managed to become a proficient, self-taught driver with only one mishap. On a rainy day, I was cruising at about 50 miles per hour on a straight blacktopped country road elevated about 4 feet above a farm field. I hit a small bump, the car spun off the road, and for a moment, I became airborne. The car landed on all four tires in the field. I contemplated my good fortune for a minute. Had the jeep turned over, I would have been reduced to a pancake. As it was, neither the jeep nor I was worse for wear. Actually, I was not sure about the jeep, because it was so beat up from its long war service that new damage was not readily visible. On October 9, 1945, I got my first driver's license. My place of birth noted on the license reflected my flaky status at the villa: It read *Sanborn, USA*. The change from Sambor, Poland, to this fictitious name was Hugo's brainchild.

Hugo Weisgall at the Grand Piano

My social life was active and convenient, if not terribly profound. My friend Vera, an 18-year-old vivacious Czech beauty, lived with her parents, right across the street from the villa. After running across each other a few times, we struck up a conversation and became good friends. We went out for quite a while before she told me, to my horror, that her father was an ardent communist and a colonel in the National Security Police, the equivalent of the Soviet NKVD. Vera's interests were clearly not in politics, but she had enough sense to keep our friendship hidden from her father. However, when he saw us together he was not amused, to put it mildly. It would not do to have his daughter in a relationship with someone connected with the American Military Attaché. She thought we had better break up. I agreed wholeheartedly, knowing full well what would happen if Vera's father uncovered my absence from the Polish military. We remained friends and saw each other occasionally until she married a year later.

When I think about it now, Hugo Weisgall was an unusual candidate for the office of Assistant Military Attaché, considering his lack of military experience. Born in Czechoslovakia and a descendent of four generations of synagogue cantors, he came to the U.S. in 1920 with his parents. He lived in Baltimore and studied music and art. During World War II, he was the U.S. Assistant Military Attaché to the Czechoslovak government-in-exile in London, and so inherited his job in Prague. For me, Hugo was a great teacher of English. He did not just correct my grammar, but as a musician he had the talent of musically mimicking and correcting my speech patterns. The fact that I speak today with relatively un-accented English is a testimony to his influence.

When not at the U.S. embassy, Hugo's big project in Prague was conducting Giuseppe Verdi's opera *La Traviata* at the Prague Opera House, which dates back to the days of Mozart. Hugo held vocal rehearsals at his villa and he accompanied the singers on the piano. The classic vocal numbers from the opera were rehearsed over and over again and are still imbedded in my brain.

On the diplomatic front, there were frequent dinners at the villa. One very memorable guest was Jan Masaryk, the foreign minister of Czechoslovakia. He was a bespectacled, bald, kind-hearted man with a great sense of humor. At the time, Czechoslovakia was the key link in moving the remaining Jews out of Poland and other communist-occupied countries into DP camps in the U.S. zone of occupied Germany. To a large extent, Jan Masaryk was responsible for allowing their unrestricted transit through Czechoslovakia. This massive undertaking was organized and at least partially financed by the Joint Distribution Committee (JOINT), an American-Jewish organization headed in Prague by a Mr. Jacobsen, another frequent guest at Hugo's dinners. I am not sure who was actually responsible for allowing the flow of refugees into the U.S. zone, but since Hugo's office was in charge of permits, I suspect he might have helped it along. From the U.S. zone, the refugees were illegally shipped to Palestine, defying the British policy of restricted immigration. No one could have imagined then that within a few years, Masaryk would be dead under mysterious circumstances.

I used to run errands for Hugo to Mr. Jacobsen and between JOINT and the border transit points. The JOINT office in Prague was located near a medieval Jewish quarter and I got to know this part of Prague quite well. There was a memorable synagogue there, where the religion, history, and tradition of Jews were so palatable that it made a lasting impression on me. The synagogue was built around the middle of the 13th century. One had to climb down stairs from the street level to bridge the centuries and enter the synagogue. It was originally called the New Synagogue to distinguish it from an even older house of prayer that did not survive. The term "old" was added to the name in the 16th century, so it is now called the Old-New Synagogue. It is the oldest surviving European synagogue in which services are still held. An ancient rabbi of this synagogue supposedly created a living man out of clay called the Golem. A statue of the Golem of Prague, said to have protected the ghetto from pogroms, still stands at the entrance to the city's Jewish sector. It is also a matter of record that this rabbi enacted a ban on entering the attic of the Old-New Synagogue, supposedly because the body of the Golem rests there to this day.

The year I spent at Hugo's villa was not all bliss. My adjustment to comfort and safety was far from smooth. I often lay sleepless at night in my comfortable bed after awaking from nightmares. I wondered why living under my true identity and staying put in one place were so frightening and disturbing to me. I craved the adrenalin rush that danger brought. I kept my problems to myself and I hoped they would go away in time.

In that summer of 1945, I applied for a visa at the American Embassy to immigrate to the United States. Immigration laws in the United States were based on quotas. Since Poland was my birthplace, I came under the small Polish quota. Many Polish Hasidic Jews would get a "clergy" preference under the quota because their organization provided them with "rabbinical" appointments in the States -- delaying others.

In 1946, with Hugo's recommendation, I received a scholarship from Stanford University. However, the U.S. Consulate refused to grant me a student visa, because as an immigration visa applicant, I was not a bona fide student. I lost the scholarship. It would be four years before my turn came for a visa in 1949. It was a four-year wait that almost cost me my life.

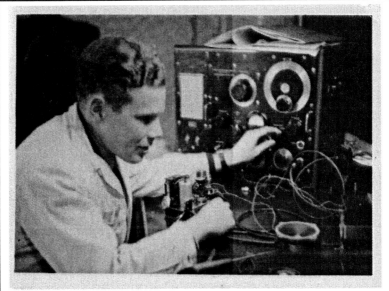

At my workbench in the lab at Tesla

By the late autumn of 1945, the villa was pretty well organized and furnished and my duties there were minimal. I asked Hugo if he minded if I got an outside job. He had no objections, as long as I would still be available if he had a task for me. My great interest since childhood was electronics, so I applied for a job with Telefunken, a German firm before the war that became Tesla under Czech management. I worked as a technician with a group designing commercial broadcast radios and I loved the work and the steady pay. I also passed an entrance exam, in lieu of a high school diploma, and enrolled in the electro-technical engineering department of Prague Polytechnic and took a course in mathematics and drafting. The education was free.

One day on the way to school, I stopped at a pharmacy to get toothpaste. Pharmacies at this time and place were not self-service and as the pharmacist handled my order, the phone on the counter rang. He answered it and started speaking with his wife in Polish. After he hung up, we found out to our mutual amazement that we were both from Drohobycz. His name was Weinfeld and he insisted that I visit on Sunday afternoon and meet a few survivors from Drohobycz who lived in Prague. I accepted and met with my compatriots on a fairly frequent basis.

The most interesting of them was Sam Rothenberg, the man who refused to join the Judenrat. He was close enough to the Judenrat to fill me in on their motivation and thinking. Sam's letter to his family describing the destruction of the Jews of Drohobycz was published in 1984 by his son-in law Edmund Silberner of the Hebrew University in Jerusalem. In it, all that Sam said on the subject of the Judenrat was: "This institution was the saddest page in Jewish history." I can understand and sympathize why he found it so difficult to talk about this issue. Yet I believe history lost a valuable witness because of Rothenberg's stature and his knowledge of, and independent position from, the Judenrat.

As soon as foreign postal service was restored in Prague, I wrote to my aunt Nettie in Philadelphia and my Aunt Regina in Tel Aviv. I

Student ID from Prague Polytechnic

informed them of my whereabouts and asked them for any news they might have about my father and sister. Late in November 1945, the answers arrived. My sister Dvora and her husband survived the war in the USSR. They returned to Poland and from there managed to get to the U.S.-occupied zone of Germany. Tova and my half-brother Anatol also ended up there. I got their addresses in displaced persons' camp and, subsequently, in 1948 visited them there. The news about my father was not what I had longed to hear. My aunt Regina sent me the very last message received from him in the spring of 1942. The purpose of the note, hand-written on an undated scrap of paper, was to tell my aunt Clara his address: 145 Red October Street in a town near Dzambul. They were both in Kazakhstan at the time.

I wrote to Kazakhstan and made inquiries. There was no record of him. No one had ever heard from my father again. There was a strong likelihood, almost a certainty, that he was dead. This hit me hard. I was close to him. I had hoped throughout the war that we would find each other again. Now, any hope of resuming family life as I remembered it was lost forever.

I kept searching to find something definitive about my father, to get closure. Finally in 1960, after years of searching, I located Dr. A. Wiesenberg in Tel-Aviv, an M.D. who was with my father in Russia, and I managed to find out from him the details of the last year of my father's life.

As I mentioned much earlier, in another lifetime really, I said my goodbyes to my father at the train station on June 25, 1941. He had been drafted into the Red Army. He left our town of Drohobycz with a field hospital and was sent to the Russian-German front. At the time the Red Army had been retreating in chaos and the Germans had more or less destroyed the unit to which the hospital was attached.

In July, 1941, he was ordered to report to Artomovsk, inside Russia on the Azov Sea. As a former Polish citizen, he took the opportunity, and all of the risks which such a step involved, to enlist in the Anders Polish Army in Russia. He was sent to Buzuluk and then to Tockoje, deep inside Russia, where the Polish Army was being formed. At the end of December, 1941, he received orders to go to Tashkent, Uzbekistan. He was sent there to fight an epidemic of typhoid fever rampant among the amnestied Polish former deportees who were concentrated there by the Soviets. Food and water-borne bacteria transmit typhoid fever and, in the days before antibiotics, typhoid fever had a high mortality rate. This assignment in Tashkent had nothing to do with his specialty of dental surgery, but called on his general medical training. His next similar assign-

Dear colleague:
I would like to ask you a great favor: Please give my address to Mrs.
<u>Clara</u> <u>Nacht</u>. I would like to ask her to tell me about her life and if
Elias joined them. I thank you very much and send regards to your wife.

Dr. Langberg
My address: Dzambul oblast, Kyrgayski rayon, Tesprevka, 145 Red
October St.
For doctor Z.L.

The last note from my father

ment was in Dzambul, in southern Kazakhstan, part of a team taking care of some 100,000 deported Poles in a camp, in the most miserable of circumstances, with mass starvation and a lack of sanitation.

In April, 1942, the Russians began to re-arrest and deport to the north a great many of the formerly amnestied Poles. To save medical officers from deportation by the Soviets, the Polish Army tried to get the uniformed medical officers back from Dzambul, to their units. My father got the orders to go to Tshok-Pak on the Soviet-Afghan-Chinese border, but before he managed to get there he contracted typhoid fever. He died in May, 1942. He was dead before I had even left the ghetto. I never found the exact date of his death or the place of his burial.

Chapter 24:

Alleluia Boy: The Last escape

In the spring of 1946, both Hugo and T.K. left for the United States. They were being discharged from the service. I knew that Hugo would return to the villa after he was discharged, but I figured it was time for me to go out on my own. I moved into a rented room, and what I lost in luxury, I gained in independence.

Hugo managed to keep his diplomatic status at the embassy and the villa in Prague by switching jobs from Assistant Military Attaché to Cultural Attaché. He returned to Prague with his wife in the autumn of 1946 and continued to live at the villa for another year or so. After returning to the States, Hugo later became a composer of modern operas of some renown. Our paths rarely crossed.

My second and third years in Prague, 1946 and 1947, were happy and uneventful. I supported myself in a modest style on my salary as a radio technician. I liked Prague and I liked the Czech people very much. Their love of music was catchy; opera in Prague was not for snobs but a popular form of entertainment for everyone.

I soon met a pleasant 25-year-old woman named Marianne, who worked at the JOINT offices. Her husband had been killed by the Nazis during the war. We spent a lot of time together in her small but comfortable apartment, playing house. She was my lover, my good companion, and my friend. My adjustment to normal life was becoming much better.

My co-workers at Tesla lab: I'm wearing the white coat. Franta and Jirzi are on my left.

Czechoslovakia was a free country. This made me very comfortable. There were no foreign troops. And even better, pictures of Stalin were limited to the offices of the Communist Party. I knew that I would have years to wait for my visa to the States and Prague was as good a place as any to stay.

I continued to work for Tesla Telecommunications as a radio technician. The Company moved to a larger, well-equipped lab on the outskirts of Prague. It was an easy trolley commute for me each day, either from my apartment or Marianne's. I worked closely with three other fellows in our unit. We were all technical-minded and in our twenties, and we got along surprisingly well. But the similarities ended there. Each one of us came from a different corner of the political spectrum.

First there was Igor, a slim, chain-smoking fellow, born in Prague to a White Russian family who had escaped the USSR after the communist revolution in 1917. Next, there was Jirzi, a round-faced, balding, good-natured communist who laughed a lot and was the shop steward for production workers. And finally, there was tall and lanky Franta. Like me, he served in the air force during the war, but with a Czech squadron in the RAF, in England. After the war, he returned to Prague with his English bride, Lucy.

Jirzi was our favorite target of political discussions. He swallowed the communist "workers' paradise" slogan hook, red line and sinker. I tried to convince him political systems should be judged by what they do, not by what they say, but I never got very far. Jirzi was a decent guy and I'm sure he had plenty of opportunity to regret his naiveté in the years that followed. The fact that we could have these discussions at all, without worrying too much about the consequences, showed we were enjoying freedom and democracy. But this would not last.

In 1947, the political clouds began to darken. The United States announced the Marshall Plan, offering substantial American help to the devastated economies of Europe. Of course, the benefit of joining the Marshall Plan was clearly evident to the Czechoslovak government, although the Marshall Plan infuriated Stalin. He felt it was an American attempt to undermine his influence in Europe. In July 1947, at a meeting with Stalin, Jan Masaryk was the lone member of the governmental delegation with the courage to oppose Stalin's view. Uncle Joe was not amused. He felt it was time to end the democratic experiment in Prague.

I could sense the gathering storm and tried to somehow accelerate the issue of my U.S. visa. I wrote to one of the American POWs that I had helped near Berlin at the end of the war. Hans Schwarzkopf promptly sent me an affidavit. I called on the U.S. embassy hoping the political situation and the affidavit would help accelerate my visa. I got the same old line: "You have to wait your turn on the Polish quota."

By January, 1948, the signs of struggle were all around us. The media, now in communist hands, were screaming for vigilance against "Western imperialists." There were Czech troops in the streets. Since Franta's wife was British, they had no problem returning to England. We had a depressing farewell party for them. I would miss Franta and I surely wished I were going with them.

In February, 1948, there was a communist coup d'etat in Prague. The pro-Soviet Czechoslovak government of Klement Gottwald took over. The first act of the new communist government was to close the borders and start arresting political opponents. Jan Masaryk was found dead below the window of his flat in Prague's Cernin Palace. Was the pro-Western foreign minister, who argued with Stalin, pushed, or did he jump? No one is quite certain, even to this day, but I would bet on the push. The charming guest I had met at Hugo's villa dinner parties was gone. The last independent government in Eastern Europe had become Stalin's puppet. The iron curtain came crashing down on the imprisoned Czechoslovakia.

A huge picture of Stalin now hung in our lobby at work. Stalin was back sneering at me. A few days later, I received a phone call at work. It was Vera. She wanted to see me. I suggested lunch or dinner. No, she said, she had to see me right away. I agreed to meet her at the trolley stop near my lab.

When I first caught sight of her, Vera was pacing up and down and ringing her hands. She looked around nervously when she saw me and gave me a quick peck on the check. She cut short any niceties: "Ed, listen carefully. I will make it short. I don't want anybody to see me with you. You will be arrested soon. Get out of the country." "Why, Vera? Slow down," I interrupted, trying to calm her. "Tell me what happened."

"It's my father," she gulped. Vera's nervousness almost made her breathless. "He found out that you are still in Prague. He rants all of the time about your activities at the Military Attaché's villa. He knows where you work. He thinks that you are an American mole. Get out, Ed, before it's too late!"

Before I could open my mouth again, a trolley screeched to a stop where we were standing, and Vera quickly boarded it. I could see her looking at me with her shoulders raised and her hand covering her mouth, as the trolley rattled away. Before I knew it, she was gone. I walked mechanically back to the lab, trying to absorb what I just heard. In the lobby, the sneer on Stalin's face looked more pronounced. I could hear him say, "Now, Langberg, I will really get you."

I stumbled back to my lab and plopped on my chair, staring blankly at the desk. Igor came over and whispered, "Ed, you look like you saw a ghost; what happened? Do you want to talk?" "Yes, Igor," I replied. He grabbed his cigarettes and pointed towards the door. We walked along the corridor. "Ed, are you in trouble?" I nodded. Igor puffed on his cigarette.

"Is it political?" I nodded again.

"Can I help, Ed?" I mustered the courage to ask him if I could stay at his place for few days. "When do you want to come?" he whispered. "The sooner the better," I whispered back. He puffed heavily on his cigarette and gave me his key.

I then went to the office of my boss who was a nice man in spite of his military sounding last name: "Mr. Major, I don't feel well. I would like to go home." "Go ahead, Ed," he said, as he looked up over his reading glasses at me. "And take care of yourself."

My long ride on the trolley gave me the chance to tackle my feelings of panic. "Ed," I gave myself a pep talk, "you have gotten soft! This is no worse than the ghetto. This is no worse than crossing the front line. It's like jumping off a train. Once you've done it, you can do it again. You should be smarter and tougher now that you are almost 23, not a 16-year-old kid. Shape up!" I searched and found the button in my mind that pushed fear out of my consciousness and shoved it deep where it could not interfere with my survival. I welcomed the familiar adrenaline rush that replaced the panic. My budding adjustment to normal life was discarded right there and then.

I got off the trolley a few stops before my building. I bought a small backpack and I continued to walk down the street towards home. I cautiously approached the apartment house where my room was. All appeared to be normal. I crept up to my room and quietly entered. I breathed a sigh a relief with my back against the closed door. Then I ran to the drawer of the night table where I had my meager savings. I quickly stuffed the envelope that held the money into my pocket. I shoved all of my papers and photos into the front pocket of the backpack, pausing for the touch of the soft velvet cover of my grandmother Sara's diary. The touch gave me confidence. "I shall survive." I hastily threw a few necessities from my wardrobe into the main opening of the backpack. I took out my key and put it on the table for the landlord. I grabbed my most valuable possession, a multi-band Telefunken radio, and left.

Igor's apartment was small, dark, dirty, and smelled of stale smoke, and I was ever so grateful to be there. As a token of my gratitude for letting me stay I would give Igor my multi-band Telefunken radio. That night, Igor asked no questions. My plans for escape were starting to take shape. To my surprise, I slept well on Igor's rickety sofa, just like in the bad old days.

The next day, I went to the U.S. Embassy for help. After all, my association with Hugo and his cronies was the source of my current problem. By this time, Hugo had long gone to the States, since his tenure as a Cultural Attaché lasted only about a year. The embassy was very likely under surveillance, but I didn't care. There were a few Czech policemen in front, but no one prevented me from entering. I asked to see the Military Attaché.

After being shuffled around a bit, I was interviewed by what I assumed to be a CIA spook by the name of Donovan (perhaps a relative of the famous General Bill Donovan, head of the Office of Special Services, the predecessor of the CIA). Donovan was a clean-

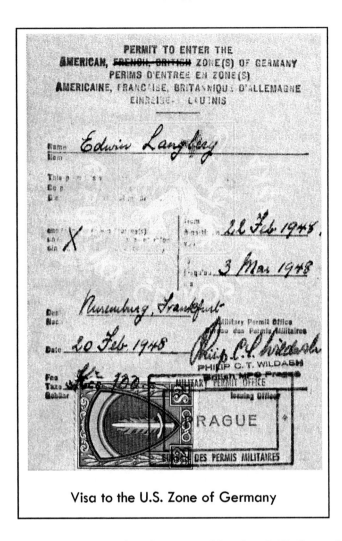

**PERMIT TO ENTER THE
AMERICAN, ~~FRENCH, BRITISH~~ ZONE(S) OF GERMANY
PERMIS D'ENTREE EN ZONE(S)
AMERICAINE, FRANCAISE, BRITANNIQUE D'ALLEMAGNE
EINREISE-ERLAUBNIS**

Name: *Edwin Langley*

From: *22 Feb 1948*
3 Mar 1948

Nuremberg, Frankfurt

Date: *20 Feb 1948*

PHILIP C. T. WILDASH

RAGUE

DES PERMIS MILITAIRES

Visa to the U.S. Zone of Germany

shaven young man, only a few years older than I. He listened to my story and then left for a while, probably to check it out. When he returned, he asked me the key question, "Ed, you weren't involved in any covert activities, were you?" No, I was just Hugo's gofer," I replied. "I ran quite a few errands for him, delivering and bringing back papers and packages, but I have no idea what was in them. Still the Commies have enough circumstantial evidence to keep me locked up for a long time." Donovan nodded in solemn agreement.

After a few minutes thinking, Donovan picked up his phone and made arrangements to get me an entry permit for the American zone of Germany.

This, of course, was the easy part; the hard part was how to get me out through the border that was now closed on the Czech side. "If you are in a real jam, I will try to get you through," Donovan promised. Considering the circumstances, this was a courageous and generous offer from him. "How?" I asked. "We would have to think about it some more, Ed. Maybe in the trunk of my car," he theorized.

"Thank you, Mr. Donovan, that's most generous of you," I said. But what I thought was: "Nice and gutsy guy, but not much experience!" I said my goodbyes to Donovan and left the embassy with my permit. I knew that before I would make up my mind, I had a real border-crossing pro to see.

That afternoon, Shlomo sat in his small office at JOINT. It was cluttered with boxes, papers, coffee cups, an overflowing trash can, and the remains of his unfinished lunch. He spoke with a clipped British accent. Shlomo was born and raised in Palestine. During the war, he fought with the Jewish Brigade on the side of the British. He was in charge of the Jewish escapee transport through Czechoslovakia. He remembered me from my earlier association with JOINT.

Shlomo listened to my story. "Bad timing, Ed," he said slowly, with a shake of his head. He proceeded to tell me that up until a few days ago, he could have buried me in a regular transport with ease. Unfortunately, with the change of the regime and the border closing, regular transports of Polish Jews to the U.S. zone of Germany were suspended. He surmised the Communists were waiting for instructions from Moscow. He was optimistic Stalin would allow transports to resume, because shipping Jewish refugees destabilized the British position in Palestine and the Middle East and Stalin liked that. "But this will take a while and you are in a hurry," he guessed. I nodded vigorously.

"Well, for really hot cargo, we occasionally use a "commercial" smuggler called Zdenek. His farm is in Domazlice, about 15 miles from the border. He is reliable and a real pro and he knows every tree on the border. For him the border is never closed." "How much will he charge me?" I feared his answer. "Don't worry, Ed. We have his services on retainer. We will take care of it. Consider it as payment for your services rendered when you worked for that Military Attaché – what was his name, Hugo something."

Shlomo told me that I would have to travel the hundred miles to Zdenek's place on my own. He gave me directions to Zdenek's farm, and warned that traveling near the border could be dangerous. I agreed. Shlomo's final instruction was to give Zdenek "regards from the Alleluia Boy, and for heaven's sake, don't dare write it down." "I wouldn't," I assured him, offended he would even think I would be that careless about a password.

Before I left, I went to Marianne's office to say goodbye. She cried. We kissed goodbye, but I didn't feel much. I was too numb. This was the price to pay for pressing the fear repression button.

The choice between Donovan and Zdenek was a no-brainer; it was going to be the Alleluia Boy. I went back to Igor's apartment and studied a map to begin my plan of departure. I decided I would travel by fast train from Prague to Pilsen. The remaining 40 miles, close to the border, I would travel either by bus, local train, or by walking. I worked out the details at the railroad station and bus depot where I obtained schedules and tickets. When I returned to Igor's apartment, I gathered my belongings and prepared for my trip.

The next morning, I thanked Igor for everything and bid him and my multi-band Telefunken radio goodbye. I boarded the Pilsen train in Prague at 6 a.m. By evening, I walked into Zdenek's farm in Domazlice completing my journey by bus and on foot. So far my plan worked without a hitch.

Zdenek was in his mid forties and married with two children. He was a bear of a man, with few words and the ruddy complexion of someone who has spent a lot of time outdoors. He owned a good-sized farm, taken from a displaced Sudeten German and given to him for services rendered in the resistance during the war. Since it takes one to know one, I wondered if Zdenek too was an adrenaline addict.

There was another "paying guest" in Zdenek's house that evening. His name was Sol, a skinny man in his thirties with black, sunken eyes. He was dressed in a business suit and appeared very protective of his suitcase. He looked more like a man waiting to catch a train at a railroad station than a man waiting to cross illegally through the Iron Curtain. I was glad when Zdenek fashioned a sling so that Sol could carry the suitcase on his back.

Zdenek told us we would make the border crossing into Germany after supper. Needless to say, Sol and I didn't eat much. Zdenek said he would get us within 500 yards of the border and tell us when and where to cross. He told us to run like hell when we reached the spot. After we crossed, he said his German partner would be waiting for us and would guide us from there. "Watch where you are going; I don't want you to fall and twist your ankle," he growled. I recognized the voice of experience. I wondered what Zdenek did with someone who could not walk in the middle of no-man's land. I did not ask. "This is your signal," he said and blew lightly on a child's harmonica. He handed one to each of us.

The night was cold and gray. Fortunately, there was no snow on the ground. The terrain was hilly and we walked mostly along wooded paths. Sol quickly tired under the burden of his cherished suitcase and Zdenek exchanged his light backpack for the suitcase. Around midnight, we stopped and had some food and a cup of coffee from a thermos. We rested for a while. Before we started up again, Zdenek gave us both a shot of schnapps, saluted in a good luck gesture, and raised the bottle to his lips and drank heartily. We walked for another half hour until we reached an open spot on the top of a hill.

The border was within sight, a bald strip of land without trees. When the moon peaked occasionally through the clouds, I could see rolls of barbed wire and long wooden posts that had been dropped off in regular intervals along the dirt road. A fence of barbed wire was being constructed, but fortunately had not yet been finished. We waited as a border patrol with barking dogs went by. I now understood why Zdenek was happy the winds were from the west. The dogs could not smell us at that distance.

Zdenek blinked his flashlight, and a response came from the other side. He motioned for us to hurry up. The three of us marched quickly towards the border. Then Zdenek abruptly stopped and pointed to a clump of pines on the other side of the bald border strip. It looked far. Zdenek gave back Sol's heavy suitcase. "Run!" Zdenek snapped in a whisper, and we made a dash for it. I ran and watched the distant clump of pines slowly getting bigger and bigger. I heard barking dogs. I ran like hell, thinking, "Don't twist your ankle, boy."

The clump of pines was getting close. I made it to the trees and slumped to the ground. A few minutes later, I heard Sol's heavy breathing. I blew my harmonica quietly and he landed heavily next to me with his suitcase pressing him to the ground. We lay there panting and waiting for a signal from our German guide.

We waited . . . It seemed like forever. We could hear the dogs in the distance. The German took his time. It was perhaps five minutes, a very long five minutes, before we heard his harmonica. Out of the darkness came Fritz, a man in his forties, wearing a ridiculous Bavarian hat. He seemed so relaxed that I expected him to start yodeling at any moment. He nodded at us and gave us the thumbs up. I had to smile.

This time we did not have far to walk to the village where Fritz's pre-war, beat-up farm truck was parked. To my surprise, the truck actually made the 50 miles to the Regensburg railroad station by dawn. Sol and Fritz squared their accounts, and from Fritz's big smile, I could tell he was satisfied. I could also tell my account was clearly settled, when Fritz shook my hand vigorously and said, "Alleluia Boy!"

We were safe! I had crossed the border with little more than what I had on my back, but I could not have been happier. Sol and I waited together at the station for the train to Nuremberg and for the first time, we really talked. I told him why I was so happy to be out of Czechoslovakia. "I am happy too," Sol smiled. "I can retire now." He carefully opened his suitcase a crack and motioned for me to peak in. The suitcase was filled with marks, World War II German currency in neatly stacked high-denomination notes. Marks were legal tender in Germany and worthless in Czechoslovakia. Sol was a smuggler, but he was a generous one. He bought me breakfast, a ticket to Frankfurt, and gave me some pocket money.

On that fateful day at Regensburg railroad station, the war had finally ended for me. I was alive, I was free, and I had a bright future. Sara's blessing came true. I had survived.

My nightmares were behind me. Well, the daytime nightmares anyway. My nighttime nightmares kept me company for a long, long time. That handy button that I used to push to keep panic deep inside me had gotten stuck. It would have helped me to know what was going on in my head, but it took decades before the term "post-traumatic stress disorder" was invented. I had to learn how to live with the old fears that were repressed inside me for so long. When they creep out at night, I can still hear the rhythmic march of German boots on the cobblestones outside my window, tak tak tak tak…

Part 5

Afterthoughts

Chapter 25

Epilogue
by Mike Langberg, *author's son*

It is more than a little ironic that my father gained his freedom by entering Germany -- the nation that had started World War II by invading Poland. One part of his life stopped on that night in February, 1948, which is why he ended his story there, although his new life had its share of both rewards and challenges.

My father sees the rest of his life as uneventful in comparison to the war years -- he would never again be in danger in the same way; never have to live under a false identity; never be without the support of family and friends; and never live in a place where it could be government policy to kill him just because of his heritage.

Yet to me, my father's life since February, 1948 is a classic immigrant success story. He entered Germany with nothing more than what he carried on his back: my great-grandmother Sara's diary, a few important papers and photographs, and a few pieces of clothing. The smuggler Sol gave him a small amount of money and bought him a train ticket to Frankfurt. These were his only material resources. What set my father apart in the years ahead were the same strengths that carried him through the war: a fierce determination to survive, a brilliant mind, and a ceaseless desire to learn and create.

So here is the continuation of my father's story:

On arriving in Frankfurt, my father stayed with family friends who had fled Drohobycz after the war. He supported himself as an electrician and radio repairman. Always confident he would eventually reach the United States, my father didn't know when his visa application would be approved. As an interim step, he decided to go to England. His friend Franta, from the Tesla radio laboratory in Prague, was now working for an English electronics company, designing television sets in the town of Aberdare, Glamorgan, in South Wales. Franta arranged for my father to get a visa for England, as well as a position with the company.

In September, 1948, the visa for England came through and my father left Frankfurt. He would spend slightly less than a year in Aberdare, the rainiest part of the United Kingdom. Looking back a half-century later, my father said he doesn't remember seeing sunshine and the green beauty of the Welsh countryside until a few days before his departure.

The long-sought visa to enter the United States came in the spring of 1949 and my father left Wales in June, sailing from Southampton, England, to New York on the ocean liner New Amsterdam. He asked my great aunt Nettie, who lived in Philadelphia, not to meet him in New York, figuring it would be inconvenient for her to make the trip. Instead, my father made his own way from New York to Philadelphia, reaching the United States without ceremony or celebration.

Nettie and her husband Hyman Rossman thought my father might want to work at their clothing stand. But my father had much bigger goals. He was admitted to the University of Pennsylvania's prestigious Moore School of Electrical Engineering and started classes in September, 1949, while supporting himself with part-time work as a technician at the school and as a television repairman on weekends.

At the age of 24, my father was now a freshman at an Ivy League university -- an almost unbelievable transformation from the adolescent who had left Drohobycz seven years before, or from the Polish Air Force soldier who had defected to freedom four years earlier. This, for me, was perhaps the biggest turning point in my father's life, other than his decision to strike out on his own in 1942. From the time he started at Penn, my father would be never anything less than an accomplished and highly educated scientist.

Passage to USA on New Amsterdam in 1949

On February 25, 1953, my father became a U.S. citizen. He graduated second in his class from Penn in June 1953 and accepted a job at RCA's research laboratories in Princeton, N.J. The job at RCA gained him entry to the graduate school at Princeton University, and he received a Ph.D. in electrical engineering from Princeton in 1956 -- completing his doctoral work in just two years.

In the following two decades, my father alternated between working for large electronics companies and starting businesses on his own; first in the Boston area, then returning to the Philadelphia area in 1970. In 1973, he decided to stick with independent consulting, and has worked on his own ever since. Through all these endeavors, he stayed on the cutting edge of technology, accumulating a lifetime total of 22 patents in electronics and biomedical engineering.

While my father was moving from one professional success to another during his early years in the United States, he was struggling inside. In 1950, my father met my mother, Meredith Stern, at Penn. They were married in September 1951. I was born in September of 1954, and my brother Jonathan in July 1955. But the marriage foundered and my parents divorced in 1958. This happened before I was old enough to remember, although I've gained some insight from talking to both my mother and father in later years. My father had a hard time living within the confines of family life and his restlessness led to impatience and irritability -- a result, I believe, of his war experiences. Yet he always overcame these demons in being a loving father to my brother and me. We spent time with him regularly throughout our childhood, and never saw or sensed his lingering internal conflicts.

Nor did my father cling to his happier memories of the Old World; he saw himself as an American before he ever came to the United States and has never expressed any desire to relive the past. He never returned to Drohobycz, which would have been impossible during the Cold War years when the town was part of the Soviet Union and closed to tourists. But even after the collapse of communism, which moved Drohobycz into the newly independent Ukraine, my father continues to see his birthplace as empty of meaning to him. The community, language and culture he knew are gone.

My father finally found happiness and stability in 1980, when he met and married Julie Kozubal. Julie, who has a master's degree in business administration, became my father's business partner and sailing partner, as well as the anchor of common sense and unconditional love he needed. In 1987, my father and Julie bought a comfortable and secluded home on a three-acre farm in southern New Jersey, overlooking a gentle creek. They now share a life together that is complete in every sense of the word.

Since settling down with Julie, my father has grown closer to his half-brother Anatol, who became a professor of statistics at the University of Haifa in Israel. Anatol and his wife Pnina, a psychologist, visit the United States frequently, often with one or more of their four children, and always spend time at my father's house.

In 2000, as he reached his 75th birthday, my father began working on this book. This was not a welcome opportunity for him to reflect on his life from the vantage point of retirement. Rather, it was a painful process he approached with great reluctance -- spurred on by his family -- that he endured only because he believes his story contains an important historical lesson that should not be lost after he is gone.

My father wrote most of the book on his sailboat
while sailing with Julie

My brother and I have honored the family members we never met and only know through my father's story. I have two nephews, Karl, born in 1988, and Samuel, born in 1986, who is named for my father's father. My wife Debbie and I became parents for the first time on August 1, 2000. We named our daughter Sara, in hopes the blessing of my great-grandmother will continue into a new generation.

Chapter 26

Genesis of My Memoir

The genesis of this memoir was a comment made by my wife, Julie, at the turn of the millennium: "Ed, if you keep quiet about your World War II years, you'll have to write your own obituary." The idea of writing my own obituary seemed like fun, in a gruesome sort of way. Most never get the chance.

I am not uncomfortable thinking about death. Death and I were intimate acquaintances in those war years that Julie wanted to know about. I had to make peace with death in order to survive. But I knew back then, whether I lived or died, I wanted my actions to have some meaning. Although my chances of survival were minimal, the choice of which way I would go was still mine.

It was not the recollection of fear or suffering that kept me quiet on this subject for a half century. I had good reason to be proud of my war record. I had refused to be a passive victim of the Holocaust and I chose to fight for my freedom. On my own at the age of 16, I escaped from a Polish ghetto in Drohobycz and traveled to Lvov. I narrowly escaped the Gestapo in Kiev; got caught and miraculously escaped again in Odessa; worked for the local underground; and finally crossed the front to the Russian line some 700 miles east of my starting point. In the Soviet Union, I joined the Polish Air Force and had my chance to fight the Nazis. After the war was over, I found myself in the Soviet sphere and had my share of problems with that regime until I crossed the Iron Curtain in 1948. I was finally free. This is what most of the book is about but it is not what took most of my mental energy and pain in writing.

Some war experiences are easy to talk about; others are painful. Painful memories, if not examined, tend to be pushed out of consciousness. Yet, they survive as ghosts, popping up unexpectedly in nightmares. So, throughout my later life, I was fascinated with trying to examine and understand the historical circumstances of the traumatic events I experienced as a young man. This memoir is written in two voices: one, of a young man in his teens recounting his adventures and the second, by the same man in his seventies, exploring the historical context of the events. I believe that one would not be comprehensible without the other.

The open public examination of the monstrosity of Nazi crimes helped provide me with a measure of emotional closure, but I never found this closure with my memories of the Ghetto. I fretted and fumed for months over those painful times before I wrote a single word. I remember a very different picture of life in the Ghetto than is typically depicted today. Nazi murderous acts were more complicated than simply Germans killing Jews. The Nazi physical destruction was accompanied and aided by a moral destruction of the Nazi-organized "Jewish Council" (Judenrat) in the Ghetto.

The gruesome colors of the Ghetto are forever engraved in my mind in their entire spectrum from weakness and treachery to strengths and heroism. Would I be considered a traitor if I wrote about my recollections, as unpopular as I know they are likely to be, or if I remained silent? I decided to write about my war years as I remembered them, for my wife, my two sons, and my grandchildren who otherwise would never know what I stood for in World War II. I want to commemorate the thousands of passive victims in my town by providing the circumstances of their deaths. I would like to shed some light on why millions of Jews obediently marched to their death. I decided to take to heart my own interpretation of the biblical urging: *And thou shall tell thy son…This is what the Lord did to me when I came forth out of Egypt. (Exodus 13: 8.)*

Writing and rewriting "The Judenrat Trap" was not an act, it was a journey. I started with the raw and bitter emotions of a 16-year-old boy who felt betrayed because the ghetto leadership selected his best friend for the very first "resettlement" to death. I felt then that the Judenrat were traitors who betrayed their brethren for promise of personal safety for themselves and their families and for illicit gains flowing, for some of them, from their power.

As I agonized about this issue, I realized that there was a major flaw in my simplistic interpretation of the events. I knew some of the Jewish Ghetto leaders personally or by reputation. They were *not* "rotten apples." In the pre-war days, they were decent people and truly the leaders of the Jewish community: Rabbis, lawyers, businessmen. I had to look myself in the mirror. To save my life, would *I* sacrifice my neighbor, my mother, my child? After you read about the circumstances of life and death in the Ghetto, try the mirror test. *What would you do?* To me this is a truly frightening question.

I am not the only one who has avoided this question for 50 years. Many ugly facts about wars tend to be whitewashed, in hopes of being forgotten by future generations. I was an eyewitness to an event now safely resting in historical limbo. Not many people today realize what life in the Ghetto was really like. The Judenrat governed the Jewish population in the Ghetto. Ordinary Jews like me had no contact with the Germans except for an occasional bullet. For a good while, Nazis provided the quotas but the individual selection of who lived or died depended on "lists" prepared by the Judenrat. To get on a safe list, bribery was rampant. The audience watching *Schindler's List* [13] must have wondered how the lucky ones got on his list, while others perished.

My memoir is not the first book to mention the collaboration of the Judenrat in Nazi crimes. Scholars such as Raul Hilberg [14], the distinguished historian of the Holocaust, as well as Hanah Arendt [15] raise a hint of this fact. On the other hand, an exhaustive treaty entitled *Judenrat* by Isaiah Trunk [16] is devoted to the premise that *the Judenrat had **no choice*** but to collaborate and so absolves them from responsibility for their deeds. Trunk's view is widely accepted in current Holocaust scholarship. I have no disagreements about the facts of the Holocaust. My disagreement is about the motivation, about the souls and minds of the leadership of the Ghetto.

". . . *the Judenrat had no choice*"--In the Ghetto days, this implied the mindset that our only chance of survival was to cooperate with the Nazis. This poisonous mindset filtered from the leadership to the general population leading to ever more shocking betrayals. This was clearly a lethal policy both on moral and pragmatic grounds. At best, it prolonged the life of Jews by a few months. In fact, it pacified the Jewish population and in the absence of opposition, it accelerated the Nazi Final Solution. Any opposition to the Nazis was dangerous in the extreme, but faced with almost certain death, any choice would have been better and more honorable. Alan Adelson's portrayal of the head of the Judenrat, Mordechai Chaim Rumkowski in the *Lodz Ghetto* [12] tells us something about the enormity of the moral disintegration there.

". . . *the Judenrat had no choice*"—Historians that propagate this view today tell us that we all failed the mirror test. They tell us that the drive to survive trumps all moral considerations and justifies cowardice and betrayal. I vehemently reject this view. Within years of the end of the war, these same Jews risked their lives without hesitation, fighting for the independence of Israel. The human spirit needs leadership and inspiration to risk all. The tragedy of the Holocaust was that the victims had neither. The Nazis launched a masterful campaign of psychological warfare that destroyed Jewish victims both physically and morally. The Nazis campaign was highly successful on both counts.

I do not raise controversy to offend or injure, but with the sincere hope that strength and healing are helped by the truth. I realize that it takes an eyewitness to dare raise the subject of the Judenrat doing Nazi bidding. I consider it my burden to do so now, before the few remaining eyewitnesses are gone. This crucial lesson of the result of yielding to corruption on one hand, and the resistance to oppression on the other, will be lost forever if we do not have the courage to recognize that historical truth is not always pretty or politically correct. My last war ghost has finally been exorcised. It is not hiding any more. I can see it clearly as it holds out a glittering mirror in its hand.

Notes

1   The names of towns and people in this part of the world have many spellings, depending on the nationality of the speaker, and on the country that owns the place at the time. In the author's childhood days, Drohobycz was a Polish town but now, as part of the Ukraine the preferred spelling is Drogobych. In the book the author picks one spelling of the name of a town or person and tries to be consistent.

2   a. While dates are based on family documents and personal notes and recollections, critical dates and the number of victims were verified in references b and c below. When the two references disagree, author's choice was based on his judgment.

b. Martin Golbert. Atlas of the *Holocaust*. Second Edition, Pergamon Press, New York, 1993.

c. William Fern (compiled by). *Brief History of the Jews of Drohobycz*. Booklet for the reunion of survivors of Drohobycz, S. Fallsburg, New York, May, 1985 (copy available at Yivo Library Archives, 1048 Fifth Ave, NYC). Fern's booklet, while quite valuable, contains a highly offensive remark on page 16. In connection with the Nazi "Resettlement" order for 1000 Jews in March 1942, Fern states: "The council (Judenrat) selects thieves and informers to fill the required quota." This is an incredible example of trying to justify the collaboration of the Judenrat with the Nazis by maligning their innocent victims.

3   Edouard Calic. *Reinhard Heydrich: The Chilling Story of the Man Who Masterminded the Nazi Death Camps*. Hippocrene Books, New York, 1988.

4   William Styron. *Sophie's Choice*. Random House, NY, 1992. Movie directed by Alan J. Pakula, 1982.

5   At the time of writing, Landau's diary was available on Internet in the original German at: http://motlc.wiesenthal.org/specialcol/instdoc/d04c07/index.html.

Notes

6   For the story of the Bruno Schulz murals, see *Artwork by Holocaust Victim is Focus of Dispute*, Celestine Bohlen, The New York Times, June 20, 2001, p. A1.

7   Wielsaw Budzinski. *Schulz Pod Kluczem* (In Polish). Grupa Wydawnicza Bertelsmann Media, Warszawa, 2001.

8   Albert Seaton. *The Russo-German War 1941-45*. Presidio Press, CA, 1993.

9   Internet advertisement of plastic model I-48022 *Warszawa Regiment*. Manufactured by ICM LTD, Box B59, Kyiv, 252001, Ukraine.

10   Josef Garlinski. *Poland in the Second World War*. Hippocrene Books, New York, 1985, p. 268.

11   Primate Hlond's statement of July 11, 1946 is quoted in Stewart Steven's *The Poles*. MacMillan, New York, 1982, p. 307; also in S. Segal's, *The New Poland and the Jews,* New York, 1948, p. 80; see also John Russell to Ernest Bevin, Warsaw, July 29, 1946, British Public Record Office, ref. no. FO 371/56444.

12   Henryk Grynberg. *Drohobycz, Drohobycz*. Wydawnictwo W.A.B., Warszawa, 1997.

13   *Schindler's List*. MCA/Universal Pictures 1993. Screenplay by Steven Zaillian. Based on the novel by Thomas Keneally, directed by Steven Spielberg.

14   Raul Hilberg. (a) *Perpetrators, Victims, Bystanders: The Jewish Catastrophe 1933-1945*. HarperCollins, New York, 1992.

(b) *The Destruction of European Jews*. Holmes & Meier, New York, 1985.

15   Hanah Arendt. *Eichman in Jerusalem: A Report on the Banality of Evil*. Penguin Books, New York, 1996.

16   Isaiah Trunk. *Judenrat: The Jewish Councils in Eastern Europe under Nazi Occupation*. University of Nebraska Press, Lincoln, 1996.

17   Alan Adelson and Robert Lapides (compiled and edited by) *Lodz Ghetto*, Viking Penguin, New York, 1989.